Calligraphy Techniques

The Essential Step-by-step Beginner's Guide to Calligraphy

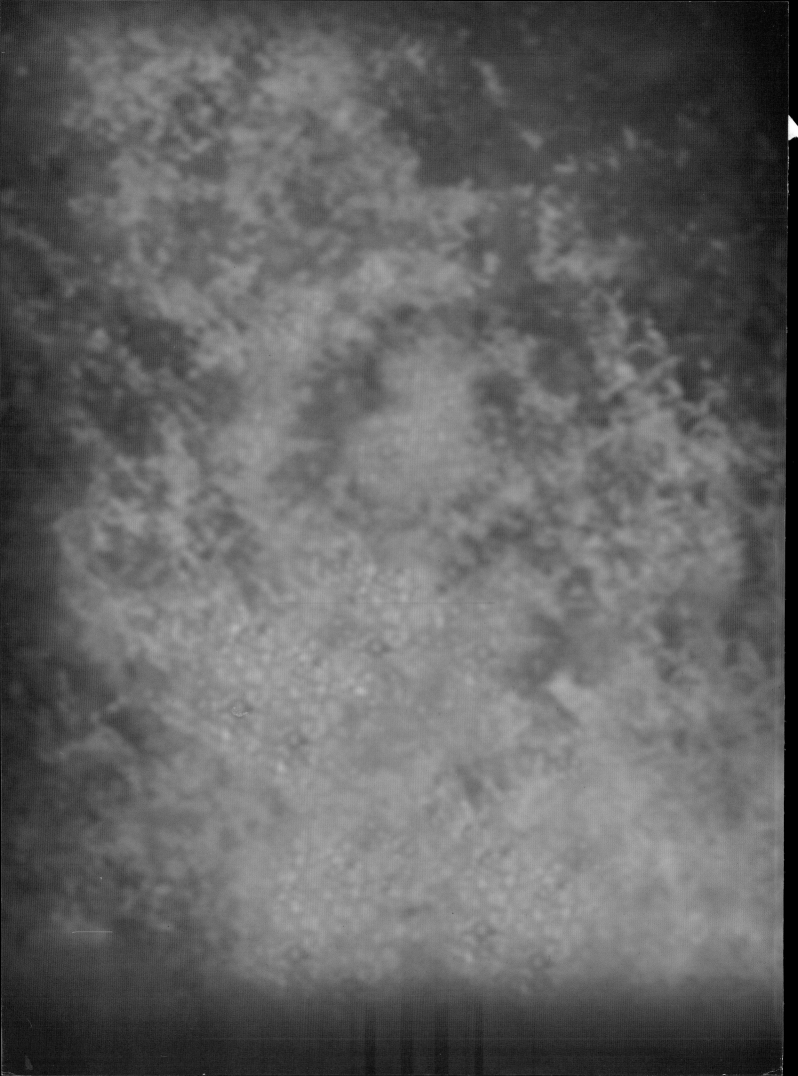

Calligraphy Techniques

The Essential Step-by-step Beginner's Guide to Calligraphy

Mary Noble

BARNES
& NOBLE
BOOKS
NEW YORK

ABOUT THE AUTHOR

Mary Noble is a freelance calligrapher who has many years of experience in teaching her skills to adults. She has exhibited widely, and has written several books about calligraphy, notably with Janet Mehigan. She is a Fellow of the Society of Scribes & Illuminators and also of the Calligraphy & Lettering Arts Society, of which she is currently Chairman.

This edition published by Barnes & Noble, Inc.,
by arrangement with Bookmart Limited

2003 Barnes & Noble Books

First published in 2001 by Bookmart Limited
Desford Road, Enderby
Leicester LE19 4AD
England

M 10 9 8 7 6 5 4 3 2 1

ISBN 0-7607-3875-0

Printed in Singapore

Text and calligraphy examples by Mary Noble
Calligraphy and text for 'Versals' by Janet Mehigan
Designed by Sue Pressley and Paul Turner
Edited by Philip de Ste. Croix
Photography by Roddy Paine
Manuscripts on pages 10 and 11 by permission of The British Library.

AUTHOR'S ACKNOWLEDGEMENTS

I am grateful to my husband Julian for his support, to Janet Mehigan whose Versals are so much better than mine, to Gaynor Goffe for teaching me much of what I know, to Peter Thornton for critical comments, and to my friends Jan Pickett, Ros Pritchard, Janet Mehigan, Georgina Guest and Jane Gilbert for the calligraphy pieces featured on pages 157–160. Thanks to Fareham Gallery for lending items for display, and to Sue Pressley for demonstrating the techniques for photography.

CONTENTS

INTRODUCTION

Observers who know that I am a calligrapher are shocked to find how untidy my everyday note-taking is. I use a ballpoint pen like most people, and as long as I can read what I have written, that's fine by me.

When writing to a friend, I tend to take more care, keen that my writing should both be readable and look good on the page. I sometimes choose a narrow fibre-tip pen as it has more 'drag' than a ballpoint, and makes me write more slowly.

When it comes to calligraphy, that's slower still. Now I take great care with every letter, using a broad-edged pen and striving to make all the letters look as if they belong to a matching set – almost as if they were part of a type font. But not so much like a font that I might as well type the letter out on the computer! Indeed, there are fonts available that exploit that 'hand-made' look so cleverly that sometimes you are not sure of their origin; if they are very beautiful, then you can be sure that they were designed or adapted from a hand-drawn original.

The attraction of using calligraphy is that it allows us to produce something that both looks beautiful, and proclaims itself to be hand-made. There is a definite sensual pleasure for the writer in making rhythmical movements with a pen; the fact that these marks represent words gives us the motivation to use the technique frequently. For the reader, the pleasure is in appreciating the beauty of the completed work. And in between those two, as I know from teaching my classes, lies the fascination of the performance, of watching a calligrapher write!

Try it for yourself. Accept the fact that you will not become expert in a couple of weeks. As with all skills, you need to practise regularly, and to develop an eye for accuracy. Stick with one alphabet style until you can reproduce it without constant reference to a book, before you try another. Never get stuck on one letter – give it three attempts, then move on to other letters and come back to it later. The experience of creating the other letters will help you to shape that first one again, but this time better.

Practising is important, but employing calligraphy to make something is better still. That way you get to practise while you also create an end product. The motivation of having to prepare, for instance, some labels for a friend will encourage you to finish the job, when otherwise you might have let the whole project slide.

So, ignore the scruffiness of your note-taking – and mine too – and resolve to accept calligraphy as a separate branch of writing; one that's slower, more graceful, and more carefully crafted. It is writing for special occasions, to be enjoyed both by the writer and the reader alike.

Through & through

GREAT POWER IS OURS

such that all Creation,
in all things, stands by us

THE EARTH
should not be injured

THE EARTH
should not be destroyed

HILDEGARDE of BINGHAM

HOW IT WAS

We generally take all the modern art materials and tools
which are available in art shops around the world for granted.
Yet it is only during the last century that such items have
become readily available. Paint in tubes, metal pens,
ready-made inks, machine-made paper, all of these
are recent inventions.

However, we do still look to the past for ideas and skills to inspire us – for example, the quill pen used on vellum is still revered by many professional calligraphers.

PAPYRUS

This is not a very smooth surface on which to write, but it gave good service to the Ancient Egyptians for thousands of years. It is made from thin layers of the fibrous inner part of a plant stem laid in strips, with a second layer positioned crossways, then hammered flat and dried under weights. The Egyptians used soft reed brushes (made from fraying the end of a dried reed stem, not a hollow one like a pen) to write on this surface.

VELLUM AND PARCHMENT

Animal skin eventually supplanted papyrus as the writing material of choice, and is still in use today by calligraphers for prestige works. Calfskin vellum is the preferred material, ideal for use with the quill. A lengthy process of soaking in lime, scraping, stretching and drying produces the creamy-white skin. The making of these skins was in greatest demand in the Middle Ages, when illumination was at its height, and

book production was trying to keep pace with growing literacy. It is thanks to the durability of the skins that such beautiful books remain in existence. Today, vellum is used for scrolls of honour, specialist bookbinding, and works which include raised gilding. For framed work it is often stretched round a board to keep it flat, as it is sensitive to changes in humidity.

REED PENS

These are quickly cut from the hollow stems of reeds, and nibs are fashioned to a shape on which our

modern-day metal pens are modelled, with a curved shaping, flat edge and slit. The nib of a reed pen softens rapidly with use, so the writer needs to change them regularly. Reed pens were still in common use in the West until the sixteenth century.

QUILL

Longer-lasting than the reed pen, the quill is cut from the flight feathers of a goose or swan. Turkey feathers are often used today according to availability. It is cut in the same way as a reed, but stays sharper for much longer. When used on the smooth surface of vellum, the quill glides across the page effortlessly, making light work of flourishes.

PAINTS

Medieval painters were obliged to grind their raw powdered pigment and mix it with water and a glue to make it adhere when dry. Many years of apprenticeship were needed to develop the requisite expertise in obtaining the right consistency, and avoiding it cracking or dusting off when dry. These were everyday concerns and we must be grateful in the present day that we can leave them to paint specialists.

Furthermore, many of the pigments were hazardous to health, using such substances as white lead, arsenic trisulphide (orpiment yellow), and mercuric sulphide (vermilion).

INKS

Various methods were developed for making writing inks. Many of the manuscripts surviving today look brown, suggesting their oakgall origin. Black inks were made from soot mixed with water and a gum, but these sat on the surface of vellum; the more effective inks which etched into the surface were made from crushed, soaked oak apples mixed with ferrous sulphate which turns it dark brown to black, the mixture then being sieved. The result is a watery ink which darkens after exposure to air. If used today, beware of using it with metal nibs, as it eats away at the metal and makes the pen scratchy.

CALLIGRAPHY PAST AND PRESENT

Calligraphy is an ancient art, and we are fortunate that
museums, cathedral libraries and private collections around the
world have preserved some of the best examples.

Take the opportunity, if it arises, to look closely at any historic manuscript. Admire its page layout and beauty of decoration (the usual reason that it is on display) and then study closely – using a magnifying glass, if possible – the writing in the main text. See if the style is familiar, note the shapes, and the date, for future reference.

EVESHAM PSALTER (above)
This manuscript was created some time after 1246 for an abbot of Evesham. The S is illustrated with a depiction of Jonah and a fish.

Decoration, including the most beautiful illumination, had by this time been developed into a fine art. This type of book (a psalter is a book of psalms, devotional songs for use in church) would be specially commissioned as a prestigious object, serving the joint purpose of paying homage to God and demonstrating the wealth and status of the owner.

So, admire the page layout and the decoration; note how the text fills the width of the page, and how the initial and first words command attention by taking up more than a third of the page.

Modern newspapers employ the same technique of arresting our attention, by enlivening areas of plain text with a big picture and banner headlines.

The skills of illumination are highly developed; look at the detail in the painting of the fish's scales, the raised gold with punched patterning, the decoration along the main stroke of the S. Admire the overall balance of the design, incorporating seven lines of drawn ('built-up') capitals. See how the same kinds of capitals have been used in the margin, and the fun that has been had in 'doodling' line patterns around them.

Patterning has also been used, in a more low-key manner, to fill in the ends of lines of text; this was a common device of the time; the colours are much paler here than elsewhere, so that they do not compete with the main focus on the page.

Now drag your eyes away from the decoration and study the text lettering, an area often ignored by museum visitors. The text is written in Latin, in a Gothic hand, of which there are many variants (see page 40 for a starter version). They are all characterized by their solid, close-packed rhythm of vertical stripes; this one has diamond shapes at top and bottom, except where some of the bottoms have flat feet; this version is described as textura (solid texture) prescisse (a term that refers to the care needed in the detail of making the flattened feet).

RAMSEY PSALTER, C. AD 974–986 (opposite top)
The picture shows part of a page that demonstrates three letterforms. The D is a drawn, rather than written, letter (see page 68 for how to do 'Versals'), in this case prepared in raised gold. There is evidence of damage around the letter, of unknown cause; scholars speculate

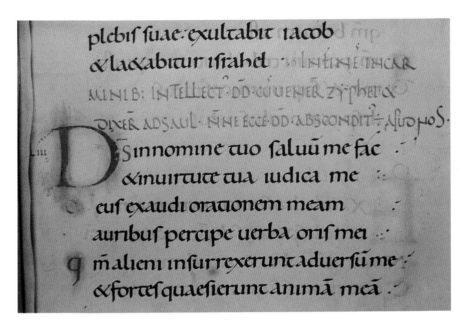

idiosyncrasy. His version is called Foundational hand (see page 32).

Calligraphers today are set free by technology; our everyday writing, correspondence, business text, records etc. can all be done swiftly from a keyboard. This leaves the lover of fine writing free to explore the beauty of the letterforms for their own sake, for creative expression and for occasions where we want a contrast to the uniformity of print.

THE PRESENT

The piece below uses several letterforms in a controlled way, to highlight the content of the text. The three focus words – Wars, Power, and Peace – have been arranged to fall centrally; the central phrase, the highlight of the quotation, is written on Japanese paper with gold flecks in it, a technique chosen to highlight the text, although in some light conditions it can obscure the writing.

that the raised medium contained an oil which has leached out, or that the vellum reveals the amount of rubbing that was done during the burnishing of the gold to make it shine.

Above the D are several lines of text in the Rustic letterform (see page 12), a capital letterform which was popular from Roman times.

The main bulk of text is in a style known as the English Caroline hand, which owes its fame among calligraphers to Edward Johnston who championed it in the early 1900s as a fine example to study because of its beauty, simplicity and freedom from

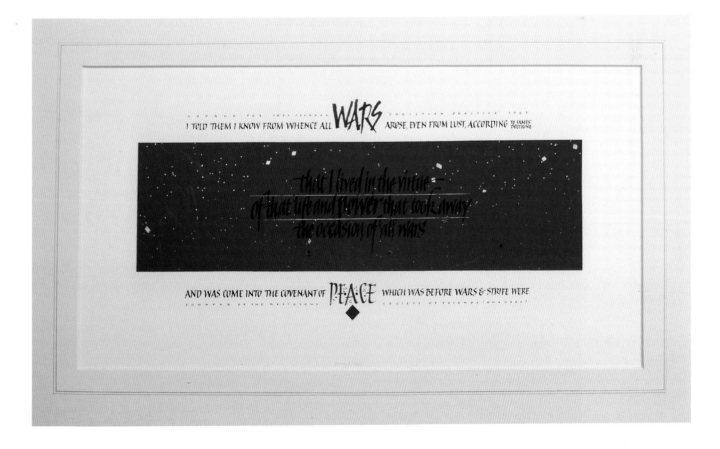

CALLIGRAPHY'S ANCESTRY

The calligraphic alphabets in this book are based on examples which have a long and respectable pedigree. There are many others; too many to include in one book. The story of their evolution is a fascinating one.

We start our story 2000 years ago, with the Romans, because their influence on Western culture and traditions is particularly evident in our system of writing. But the history of writing goes much farther back than that – the earliest evidence is Phoenician, dating from over 3000 years ago.

The Greeks apparently learned about writing from the Phoenicians, from about 750 BC; and the Romans adapted the Greeks' alphabet to meet the needs of their Latin language and speech sounds.

TRIBP

ROMAN CAPITAL

The best-known Roman letterform is the Capital, developed from the first century AD for important inscriptions; they were written with a broad-edged brush and then carved. Their classical beauty is still admired – the title typeface on this page is faithfully based on the inscription on Trajan's Column in Rome, c.AD 140. For less formal occasions, literate Romans used an everyday cursive form, speedier to write than those capitals, but few examples survive.

ᛁ QVEFVGASEC

RUSTIC CAPITALS

For pen writing, the simpler Rustic Capitals were developed in the first century AD. For at least five centuries they were used in manuscripts, on posters and occasionally in less prestigious inscriptions.

ᛁ ANIMA per me

UNCIALS

The Uncial script was brought to Britain from Rome by the missionary St Augustine in AD 597. This style became associated with the new Christianity, and the letterform spread with the demand for copies of the Bible. The script has many forms, some with much pen manipulation ('Artificial Uncial'), others much more quickly written styles.

ᛁ primus

HALF-UNCIAL (INSULAR MAJUSCULE)

'Half-Uncial' is a misleading name as it developed independently from Uncials. Insular refers to the islands of Britain and Ireland, Majuscule denotes that these characters are still seen as capitals, despite some extended strokes. They are very rounded, with a flat pen angle and usually very pronounced wedged serifs; slow, prestigious writing, from about AD 600.

ᛁ populur

INSULAR MINUSCULE

Also known as the Anglo-Saxon hand, it was in use from the end of the fifth century, often seen as a gloss (translation) in prestigious Uncial and Half-Uncial manuscripts. It looks more like cursive handwriting, but is still carefully formed, often with wedged serifs.

ignorare

CAROLINE MINUSCULES

This was named after Charlemagne, King of the Franks. His scriptorium in Tours, France developed this new script in the late eighth century for clarity, regularity and readability. It is largely based on the Half-Uncial, but with longer ascenders and descenders and a slight slope.

carbonibus

By the tenth century, the English version of this hand was more upright, rounded and with shorter ascenders and descenders.

INCIPIT

BUILT-UP CAPITALS

It became customary by the eleventh century to write bigger capitals, to give more weight to a title or the beginning of a verse. This was achieved by writing the letters with extra thickening strokes. Some forms follow Roman capital proportions; others use Uncial shapes ('Lombardic versals'). They remained popular up to the sixteenth century.

Secreta

GOTHIC HANDS

Slowly the Caroline styles became more compressed, culminating in these solid, compressed, angular letters with elaborate contrasting capitals. Gothic hands reached their full potential by the thirteenth century.

rogamus

ROTUNDA

The Italians never really took to the angular Gothic style, but instead developed their own version, known to us as Rotunda, which was more rounded and open but still with a solid weightiness. It was fully developed by the twelfth century.

a trop de ordeyne

CURSIVE GOTHIC

While the formal, slowly written Gothic hands adorned prestigious manuscripts, there was a need for a simpler, quicker version, and cursive versions evolved alongside, generically named 'bastard' scripts because of their mixed origins – a combination of formal Gothic and informal cursive.

omnes

HUMANIST MINUSCULE

In the fifteenth century in Florence, Humanist scholars looked to their forebears and found the Caroline hand; this they modified and brought up to date. Printed books were starting to appear by this time, and this script became a model for text typefaces.

quidem nom dunque

ITALIC

The Humanist script had one drawback; it was slow to write. The

Italian Niccolo Niccoli is credited with creating a cursive (joined-up) version, in 1420, that was later adopted by the Papal Chancery, hence Chancery Cursive, our first Italic hand. Typeface versions followed, but they needed each letter to be separated, and this in turn influenced scribes, who stopped joining up their letters and produced a formal Italic script.

February

COPPERPLATE

Back to joined-up writing! This is a development from Italic, but demanded a complete change of pen – using a pointed, flexible nib. It had become the script of choice in business dealings by the eighteenth century. Decorative flourishing and embellishment followed.

MODERN CALLIGRAPHY

Calligraphy largely lost its professional role once printing was established, apart from in the legal profession and all those skills disappeared for 400 years. In the early 1900s through scholarly investigation and personal skill, Edward Johnston revived an interest in calligraphy that began a new era.

The scripts most popular with present-day calligraphers are Italic, Roman Capital and Foundational; handwriting as taught in schools is often based loosely on these, too.

Today we use calligraphy for pleasure, for commercial artwork, individual designs, and as a means of personal artistic expression.

EQUIPMENT

Now it's time to collect the tools you need to help you to get
the greatest enjoyment from your calligraphy. Here are some
of the most useful items; look elsewhere in this book for
projects using them and more detailed explanations.

PENS

One handle and a full range of sizes
of nib will suffice to start. Later you
will want more handles to save
having to change nibs. There are
many makes of handle, and several
makes of nib, so check one fits into
the other!

PENCILS AND ERASERS

Keep a selection of pencils, well
sharpened, of different hardness, for
ruling lines and making sketches and
notes. Soft pencils (B, 2B etc.) are
easier to erase but blunt quickly, hard
pencils (2H, 4H etc.) can be
difficult to

erase if you press too hard. Erasers are
also soft and hard – usually a soft
plastic one will work best to erase
lines – hard erasers can damage the
paper surface.

RULER

This is essential; make sure it has
clear markings, and preferably choose
a transparent one as
the markings are

then on the underside and allow for
more accuracy. Never cut along a
plastic ruler as you will damage the
edge, unless it has a metal strip
inserted for that purpose.

INKS AND PAINTS

There are many kinds of inks and
paints which you can use either
in the dip pen or as background
washes. Fountain

pen inks are suitable for practising but not for long-term display because they fade. Choose watercolours or gouache paints for more permanent work.

BRUSHES

Choose a cheap size 3 or 4 brush for mixing paint, and loading the pen. More expensive brushes might be needed for applying paint in small areas, and you may want a wash brush for larger areas.

PAINT PALETTE

Mixing paints allows for much more variety from just a small range of colours, and so a palette with plenty of sections is an essential item. Plastic palettes are lightweight, but if staining is a concern, choose a china one.

MASKING TAPE

Buy this at car accessory or DIY stores, and use it for fixing your paper in place, padding your board, and attaching your ink bottle to the table to prevent spills. It is easier to use than plastic tape.

CUTTING TOOLS

A cutting mat has markings which help you to cut at right angles. Use it with a safety metal ruler, and a scalpel-type knife with spare blades.

COMPASS

Not essential, but useful if you need to draw a circle, or use to measure approximate widths between lines.

T-SQUARE

Small plastic T-squares are convenient and transportable; wooden ones are sturdier and usually larger. They save time in ruling all the parallel lines that are needed and can be used in conjunction with a setsquare to obtain right-angled lines.

PROTRACTOR

This is a very useful item for checking pen angles. Every alphabet you find in this book states the angle for the pen, and this angle differs with each alphabet style.

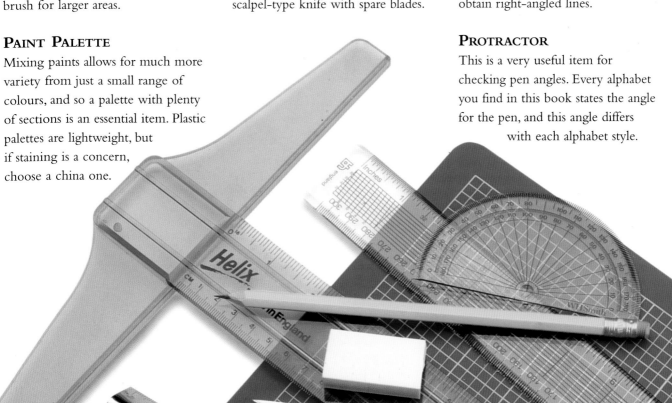

SETTING UP

Paper, pen and ink are the only items you need when you start calligraphy, but as you develop your interest and spend some time writing and designing, you also need to pay attention to your comfort. Here are some suggestions for setting up a workstation.

Writing on a flat table can cause a strain on your back; a sloping board is a better answer. The most economical solution is to obtain a piece of plywood, or other stiff wood, and to cover this with several layers of paper. Iron some newspaper then put just one white sheet of paper on top of it – blotting paper is fine if you can buy it without a crease in the centre – and fix it down with masking tape. Take care not to let the tape lap over the left-hand edge of the board, so that you will be able to use a T-square unimpeded.

Protect the tabletop with newspaper or blotting paper, and make a space on one side for your inks and pens. While you may keep most pens in a pot, the ones you are using will probably lie loose on the table; to prevent them rolling off, lay them on corrugated card.

And to keep your ink from tipping over, cut a hole in a bath sponge and squeeze the bottle in; should it leak, the drips will be absorbed by the sponge.

If you join a class in order to learn more about calligraphy, and to meet other calligraphers, you might wish to invest in a travelling kit. Keep your pens and tools in a plastic toolbox, which is easy to transport, and consider purchasing a small folder to carry your work and to keep your papers flat.

Prop up the board with a brick (wrapped in cloth to avoid damage to your table) or some books – but not calligraphy books as you may want to refer to them! Try to arrange it so that your table is in a well-lit position, preferably one that avoids you casting a shadow with your hand. A small lamp, freestanding or clipped to your board, is a worthwhile addition.

LEFT-HANDERS

Approximately one in ten people write using their left hand,
while some of them have learned to write with both hands
because they were persuaded against their natural inclination
in their early years.

Western left-handers have had it tough ever since the Romans took to writing from left to right; a direction which favours the right-hander.

The Greeks wrote 'boustrophedon' style, left to right then right to left like ploughing a field (the Greek literally means 'like an ox turning'). Chinese characters are written in vertical columns from right to left, and ancient Egyptians wrote in any direction that took their fancy.

Right-handers generally hold their pens with the handle pointing towards the elbow (see below), and move the right hand across the body to start on the left. As they write, they can see what has been written and the pen is generally pulled across or towards the body. Letter strokes usually go from top to bottom, or left to right.

A left-hander doing the same thing has to twist his or her wrist to hold the pen at the same angle.

If, instead, the left-hander chooses to hold the pen at a more comfortable angle – in a mirror image of a right-hander – most strokes will have to be pushed rather than pulled, and there is a constant hazard of smudging what has just been written. It would be more natural for a left-hander to write from right to left.

Many left-handers write with their hand hooked over, which works well with a pointed instrument, but this is not so easy when using a broad-edged pen, because the thicks and thins can occur in the wrong places, and smudging is again a hazard.

One solution, which some left-handed 'hook' calligraphers use very successfully, is to write from the bottom up – in effect following all those directional arrows on exemplars in reverse. Indeed, some people start from the right, pull up from the base, and spell backwards!

There are disadvantages, however: you are not reproducing the stroke order and direction used in the original models, for example with the upward flick of an Italic exit stroke. Thus you will not create the less formal, freer letterforms accurately because you are doing them backwards.

If you are left-handed, and you don't follow the 'hook' method (see picture above right), then some minor adjustments are all you need to write with an edged pen for calligraphy:

• Place your paper to your left, not directly in front of you, and get into the habit of moving the paper in that direction so that your hand never has to come across your body.

• Sit facing slightly to the left of your work.

• Note where your elbow is; tuck it against your side; if it sticks out, you will have to twist your wrist uncomfortably.

• Write on a raised board, so you have a better view of the area where you are writing.

Some manufacturers provide left-oblique nibs (see picture right) to help left-handers, so you don't have to twist so far. It is worth investigating what is available locally. However, the selection will inevitably be smaller, because the market is at maximum only 10 per cent of practising calligraphers.

Filing nibs to the required angle often makes them too sharp, or uneven, unless you are well practised in this technique.

You may prefer to develop the above strategies in order to be able to make full use of all the various pens manufactured for the majority of right-handers. Just remember to blame the Romans!

RULING LINES

In order to keep a consistency of writing height, and to keep
your lines straight, ruling accurate lines is really important.
There are several ways to achieve this, but in every case a
sharp pencil and accurate measuring are the keys to success.

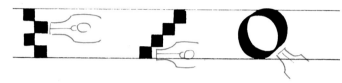

HOW WIDE?

First you need to know how far apart to rule your lines,
so start with the pen you plan to use, and the alphabet
style you want to write. Every alphabet style has its own
standard measurement, called 'nib-widths', which is the
number of times the width of the nib fits into the height
of the main part of the letter. (This is shown with each
alphabet exemplar.) That means, whether you write with a
big or small pen nib, the letters will look the same scale.

Foundational hand is four nib-widths high, so hold
your pen sideways and make squares like these, just
touching. You can do either a 'ladder' or a 'staircase', but
try to avoid the pitfalls shown here:

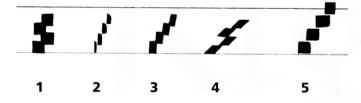

| **1** | **2** | **3** | **4** | **5** |

1 Overlapping – check the white spaces to see if they
   are the width of your pen.

2 These marks are too tentative to serve as accurate
   measurements.

3 Overlapping in the staircase method; this is the same
   problem as 1 but not so easy to spot at small sizes.

4 Wrong pen angle – you really have to work at it to
   get a totally vertical pen angle.

5 Even tiny gaps compound to make a big error.

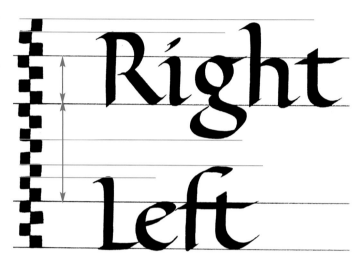

HOW MANY LINES DO I NEED?

This is where confusion can develop on a grand scale –
only rule the most essential lines. Here are ruled the
'body' or 'x' height lines, but you can see that if you
wanted them, you could also add lines for capitals,
ascenders and descenders. Don't do it! Experience shows
that the more lines you rule, the greater is the chance of
writing on the wrong ones! Instead, train your eye to
estimate accurately, noticing the following: there always
has to be a clearance gap between descenders on one line
and ascenders on the next. Ascenders in most alphabets are
a little bit taller than the capitals. Capitals are often two
nib-widths taller than the body height.

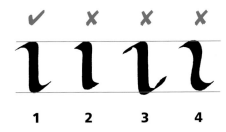

✔	✗	✗	✗
1	**2**	**3**	**4**

SERIFS

Writing between the lines usually means starting just below, and finishing with a leading-out stroke just above them. These little sideways movements create neat pointed beginnings and ends to letters – serifs – that would otherwise have blunt ends. Make sure you do them without too much over-emphasis.

1 A Foundational 'i' with serifs that are a small proportion of the whole stroke.
2 Blunt ends – not enough of a thin edge of the pen used.
3 Too much serif, so it starts and ends thick instead of thin.
4 This letter is all serif – it is over-emphasized to the extent of losing the letterform.

RULING THE LINES

If you have the equipment, the ideal method for speed is to mark the measurements down one side of the page, secure the page to a board, and use a T-square to rule parallel lines.

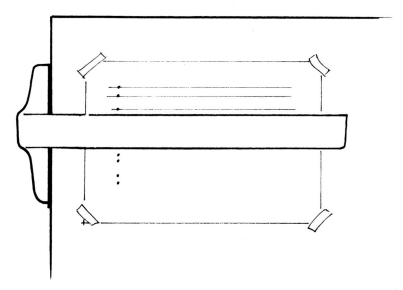

If you only have a ruler, mark the measurements carefully down both sides of the page and rule across. Do a spot check by measuring a few lines across the centre to see that they are accurate.

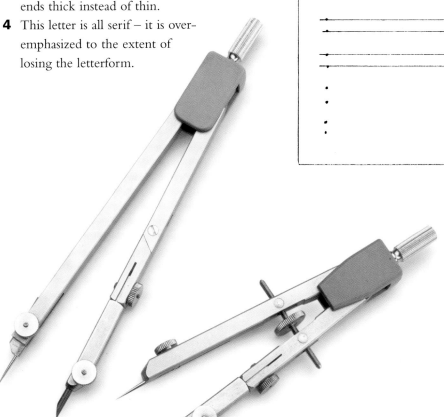

Another method is to mark the measurements on a strip of paper and then transfer these to both edges of the paper and rule across as before. This method will not be as accurate and is not recommended when working at small sizes.

Some people use a pair of dividers (which are like a compass but with two points) pricking the same measurement all the way down the page. Then you rule lines leaving out the one which allows for the double gap.

PEN PATTERNS

The edged pen is a versatile tool, and initially you may find it
helpful to play with some patterns before embarking on
a full alphabet.

The benefit to your writing in developing some of these patterns is in the rhythm you acquire from the action of regularly repeating strokes. Here are some examples you could try, and overleaf is a collection of basic shapes from which to build your own repertoire.

CREATING BOOKMARKS
Any kind of white card is suitable for these bookmarks; rule a few lines to keep the patterns straight, but don't cut them out until you have finished the patterns, in case they turn out longer or shorter than you planned. Use felt-tipped pens, or mix three colours which work well together – this colour scheme uses scarlet, an orange mixed from scarlet and cadmium yellow, and a green mixed from lemon yellow and cerulean blue. These patterns build up in complexity, so follow them in the order shown.

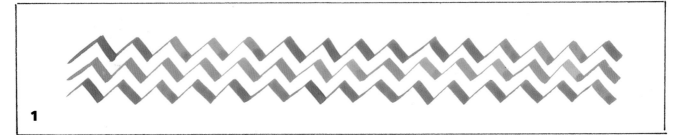

1 Three rows of zig-zags – if you are using paint, make the central row first, so you can do both green patterns without having to clean the nib again.

2 Make one row of the half-circles, turn the paper over and make the second row. Change colour, and add the diamonds.

3 As before, do one row of joined curves, then turn it over for the second row. This one has small gaps, so use a smaller nib for the squares.

4 Strong diagonal strokes, making a rope effect. Put the diamonds in when the rope is dry.

5 Another rope effect, but this time change to a smaller pen and make parallel strokes within the rope. Then outline the whole, taking care to keep a constant pen angle to preserve thicks and thins.

4

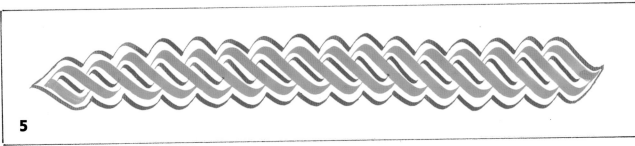

5

PROJECT

RED ROBIN CHRISTMAS CARD

You will need

CHRISTMAS CARD
- White card
- Coloured card
- Dip pen and paint/red and green ink
- Ruler, pencil, eraser
- Craft knife and cutting mat
- Small paintbrush

1 Choose sturdy white paper or card for this, and allow room for cutting and folding it into a card, or cut the design out and paste it on to coloured card.

Do your 'nib-width' practice (that's a pattern in its own right – see page 79 for a more developed pattern derived from this) to find six nibs' width, and rule a grid at that scale.

Practise the strokes which make up the robin shape, not forgetting the legs, which are made by using the pen sideways.

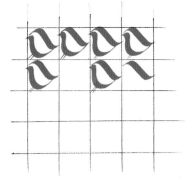

2 Put a red robin in every square except the second square on the second line.

3 Wash out your pen and change colour, or change felt-tipped pens if not using nibs and ink; make sure that the red ink is dry before you put on the green one to avoid smudging. For a finishing touch, use a small paintbrush or narrow pen to dot in tiny eyes on all the birds. Trim the paper into a small card for Christmas.

The previous pages provide some starter projects with pen patterning. If you prefer to practise before embarking on a card or a bookmark, begin here. These patterns will help you to establish a rhythm in your writing later on, and an understanding of the need for consistent pen angle. All of these, except the 'nib-width' type, are done with the pen held at 45° angle.

1

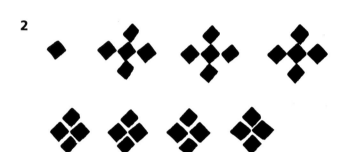

1 Hold the pen at 45° and move it sideways to get the thin hairline of the edge of the nib; then pull it diagonally for the contrasting full width of the pen. Make at least one line of this, then try adding some squares – still with the same pen angle.

2

2 Here are some more squares, or diamonds, used just on their own; make sure when copying that you keep them close together, or they lose their impact.

3

3 A curvy line combined with a diamond is a popular simple embellishment

4

4 A similar curved stroke but this time locked together in a series to form a rope effect. Try this in a narrower form and a taller form. Think about how you would turn corners if you used this for a border pattern.

5

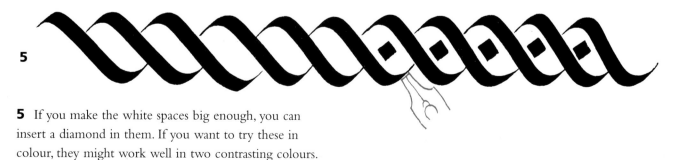

5 If you make the white spaces big enough, you can insert a diamond in them. If you want to try these in colour, they might work well in two contrasting colours.

6

6 This is the first real letter; but think of it just as a pattern and it will be easier to form. Interspersing it with a diamond makes an interesting design.

7

7 Joined curves have a lot of potential for development – try these, then put two rows together, or join a reversed row. Develop this into one of the bookmarks shown on the previous pages.

8

8 Pictorial elements can often be employed for simple and effective cards; try this flame, made in just three strokes, and here is the robin to use on the Christmas card on the previous page. However, it's interesting to note that you'll find that if you attempt a robin facing in the other direction, you will have difficulties.

9

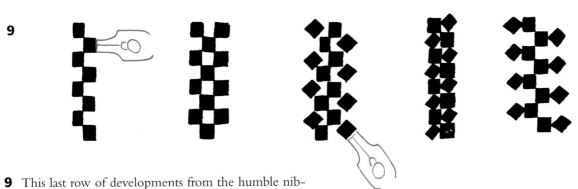

9 This last row of developments from the humble nib-width ladder is worth trying out, if only to enhance your ability to make accurate measurements for your nibs! By employing diamonds with the squares you add a livelier element – see page 79 for more of these.

THE ALPHABETS

The following 48 pages provide a solid grounding in alphabets
for calligraphy, to suit all moods from formal to decorative.

When you have become fully conversant with these, and feel ready to branch out further, the 'Script Detective' which follows on pages 76-77 shows you how to study other scripts where full information about the hands is not provided – when you see an attractive leaflet, for example, or want to study an historic manuscript for its intriguing lettering.

With regard to the alphabets provided, feel free to start anywhere that excites you. However, if you choose a difficult one for your first it may dishearten you – so leave Versals until you are fully confident with Roman Capitals, and leave Flourished Italic until you are fully conversant with the formal version.

You might try starting with Uncials if you want instant success, because they are a set on their own, with no distinct upper and lower cases.

All the alphabets are explained and introduced in the same way. There is a detailed explanation of the structural features of the letters, how to space them, a full alphabet with directional arrows included, information on how much space to leave between lines, and finally a fun page showing what calligraphers do with this style when they are fully competent.

Whatever alphabet you choose to try, make sure you start at the beginning of that section and follow it through; if you 'dip' too much in this section you will become confused.

And in case you become confused by any of the wording used, refer back here for easy explanations.

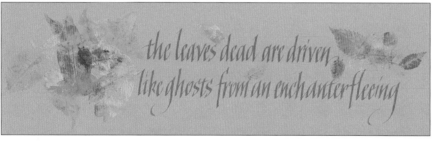

SOME CALLIGRAPHIC TERMS EXPLAINED

ASCENDER/DESCENDER
The parts which protrude beyond the body of small (minuscule) letters, such as in 'd' and 'y'.

BODY
In a small (minuscule) letter, the height not counting any ascenders or descenders. In a capital, the whole height.

COUNTERS
The spaces inside a letter.

INTERLINE
The space between the lines of writing.

LOWER CASE
The small letters – so called because they were kept in a printer's case below the capitals.

MAJUSCULE
That's the proper calligrapher's term for capitals.

MINUSCULE
The official calligrapher's term for the small letters.

NIB-WIDTHS
The number of times the thickness of a calligraphy nib goes into the body of the letter.

TRAMLINES
The top and bottom lines between which the body of the writing is positioned.

UPPER CASE
Capital letters. This is really a printer's term, referring to where the letters were kept in the trays in which type was stored.

ROMAN CAPITALS

ROMAN CAPITALS are the foundation stones of our Western writing. Their forms have survived for 2000 years, despite the attractions of many other scripts which have developed since Roman times. While you may feel familiar with the main shapes, for calligraphy you need to take note of the subtleties of their widths and proportions, which the Romans perfected, in order to make them beautiful.

The subtlety of these forms is largely determined by how each letter relates to a square or a circle. Here they are shown in related width groups.

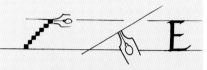

NIB-WIDTHS
The standard weight for Roman Capitals uses seven nib-widths and a pen angle of 30° from the horizontal. This angle is just enough to make the horizontal strokes thinner than the vertical strokes – best illustrated in the letters H and T. If all your strokes are same thickness, you are using a 45° pen angle, which is a common mistake.

THE HALF-WIDTH GROUP
The main portion of these letters fills half the square – but the leg of R and K sticks out a little. Note how the mid-point join in B, P and R varies in each case – B's join comes above halfway, while P is on or just below and R is definitely below that point. K is just above. This creates visual stability. The cross-bars of E and F sit on the mid-point.

THE THREE-QUARTER WIDTH GROUP
Actually, it's not exactly three-quarters – it's the width you establish when the diagonals of the square intersect with the circumference of the circle. If you have trouble gauging their width in the early stages, mark the correct width on a scrap of paper and hold it over each letter after you have made it.

Compare the upright strokes in H and N; N's uprights are inscribed at a steeper angle (60°) to provide a contrast with the thick diagonal.

THE CIRCULAR GROUP
Based on a complete circle, these letters are difficult to write at first as we tend to make them narrower than they should be. Note how little of the circle is missing from C, D and G. The cross-bar of G rises to about halfway up the vertical scale.

THE SQUARE GROUP
Strictly speaking, M is the only letter in this group! W is actually wider than the square, by half a 'V'; turn the book upside down and you will see that these letters are not upside-down versions of one another.

COMMON MISTAKES

1   **2**   **3**   **4**   **5**   **6**   **7**   **8**

1   B is top-heavy.

2   The centre stroke is too short, while the others are too long in this E.

3   Make D occupy more of the circle.

4   Raise the cross-bar in G approximately to the centre.

5   This is an upside-down W! For an M, straighten its legs.

6   Note the ugly bunching effect at the centre of the R.

7   Flatten the ends of S.

8   The pen angle has turned which makes the second stroke in V too thin

SPACING: LETTERS, WORDS AND LINES

1 Capitals need careful spacing if they are to maintain their elegance. The word 'BILL' features several upright strokes which have been positioned close together; unfortunately, no matter how closely you put the two L's, there will always be a larger space between them than exists between the I and the L. Similarly in 'LAWYER' – all the letters here are placed close together, creating uneven gaps between them.
2 When you want to check your spacing, look at it upside-down; now

the gaps are more noticeable. It helps to mark in with a pencil where you want to increase or decrease space.
3 This is better spacing; keep the L and A as close as you can, as they already have lots of their own space, move W farther away, keep Y close, and so on.

1 LAWYER BILL

2 LAWYER BILL *(shown upside-down)*

3 LAWYER BILL

The End

COMBINING CAPITALS WITH LOWER-CASE

The Roman Capital will not look out of place with any other letterform, but its most usual lower-case companion is the Foundational Hand (see pages 32-35). If you are using capitals within mainly lower-case text, then your lines should be ruled for lower-case spacing only. Gauge the height of the capitals by eye; they should be lower than the ascenders.

1 AND WHERE 'TIS FINE
IT SENDS SOME PRECI
AFTER THE THING IT LO

2 AND WHERE 'TIS FINE
IT SENDS SOME PRECI
AFTER THE THING IT L

3 AND WHERE
'TIS FINE IT SEN
SOME PRECIOUS
INSTANCE OF
ITSELF AFTER TH

SPACING LINES

When you are writing entirely in capitals, it is fun to experiment with the spaces between lines. The standard gap is the same height as the letters themselves (**1**); this aids readability, particularly in long lines of text.

If you want a closer texture to your design, try line spaces set at half the height of your letters (**2**); this spacing is standard for contemporary designs.

If readability is less important than getting a block of texture, or if you are using only one or two words per line, try writing with no gaps (**3**); make sure that you leave only minimal spaces between words or you will find big white gaps within your texture.

VARIATIONS

Once you have grasped the fundamentals of Roman Capitals, all sorts of possibilities for playing with the basic forms present themselves. Try copying some of these examples shown on the opposite page.

A Heavy (three nib-widths) and densely packed for impact.
B Double stroke – the second stroke is added with the same pen held sideways.
C Small, wide and spread out laterally.
D Chunky, with slab serifs, written on rougher paper to give texture to the letters.
E Lightweight, about 14 nib-widths high.
F Manipulated – the pen is twisted to achieve thicker and thinner strokes.
G Free – written quickly with a ruling pen.

A

B M N

C S H A K E S P E A R E

D A B C D E

E SHAKESP

F MANIPUL

G ABCDEFG

THE FOUNDATIONAL HAND

THIS SCRIPT, or 'hand', is the one most frequently used as a teaching hand for beginners, hence its title. It is plain, unadorned, and easy to read. Edward Johnston, the father of the modern revival in calligraphy in the early 1900s, gave it this name when he designed it, using as his inspiration a particularly beautiful, classic hand in a tenth-century English manuscript, the Ramsay Psalter (now in the British Library, London).

It is written fairly slowly, with several strokes to each letter; note how the shapes of the letters 'a' and 'g' are much more familiar to us as type than as handwriting.

This is a popular hand for formal projects, and occasions which demand plain text.

Use the Roman Capitals with this hand (see pages 28-31).

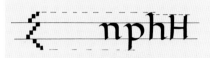

NIB-WIDTHS

Rule lines at four nib-widths high for the body of the letter. Note the heights of ascenders, descenders and capitals, but do not rule all these lines! Use your eye to judge. Just rule 'tramlines' for the body height, and set these tramlines twice the body height apart. The pen angle should be approximately 30° from the horizontal.

ocepqbd gs

nmhar u lt ιjk

vwxyz n a t e

LETTER SHAPES

Try copying the letters that are most similar to each other in groups, as shown. Note particularly the 'o' shaped letters and the arched ('m', 'n' etc.) letters.

The letter O is the governing shape for most of the alphabet, so make sure you think of O when you write; if you do, the arch in 'n' will

join very high up, and the bottom shape of 'a' will be in line with its 'roof', and 'e' will not be too narrow – these are all common errors to avoid.

COMMON MISTAKES

1   2   3   4   5   6   7   8

1 Keep the 'roof' of 'a' as wide as the base; the top stroke should be the same as in 'n'.

2 Flatten the top curve in the bowl of 'd' to avoid too much thickness.

3 Open out the white shapes to make it more rounded – flatten top and bottom end strokes.

4 Wrong angle, give 'e' more curve and flatten the angle of the thin stroke.

5 Arch starts too low, giving it a weak join.

6 Good arch, but a weak serif at the starting stroke.

7 Make the 'r' stroke as you would when starting an 'n'.

8 Don't forget the final top stroke; this is an elegant tail, but you may not have room for this much in general usage.

SPACING LETTERS

Some letters come with space attached to them, like 't', 'r' and 'a'; take pity on those which don't, like 'i' and 'n', and be generous on their behalf. Look what happens if you don't – in the top line 'r' and 'a' together pool their space and make it enormous, while next door the 'n's' and 'i's' are closely packed. You need to even out the spaces by packing 'r' and 'a' close together and spreading out the others.

LINE SPACING

The standard gap between lines for the Foundational hand is twice its body height. This leaves plenty of clearance for the ascenders and descenders; it also allows the eye to travel comfortably along lines of text, so you could write ten-word lines without impairing readability.

For short designs it is sometimes necessary to reduce the space between lines of writing, but beware of potential clashes between ascenders and descenders, and keep the lines short.

VARIATIONS

When you are thoroughly familiar with the Foundational hand, you could try copying a few of these variations shown on the opposite page:

1 Lightweight: write it with more nib-widths than the norm; this takes a steady hand.

2 Written using an automatic pen, with a flick of the edge of the nib for lightweight serifs.

3 Contrasting light and heavy weights; this works best if the words are pushed close together.

4 Compressing laterally (and with a second colour dropped in while wet).

5 Chunky letters with wedge serifs to create a sturdy look.

6 Lightweight and expanded (and with a colour change).

7 Tall and squashed: take care not to let it become italic.

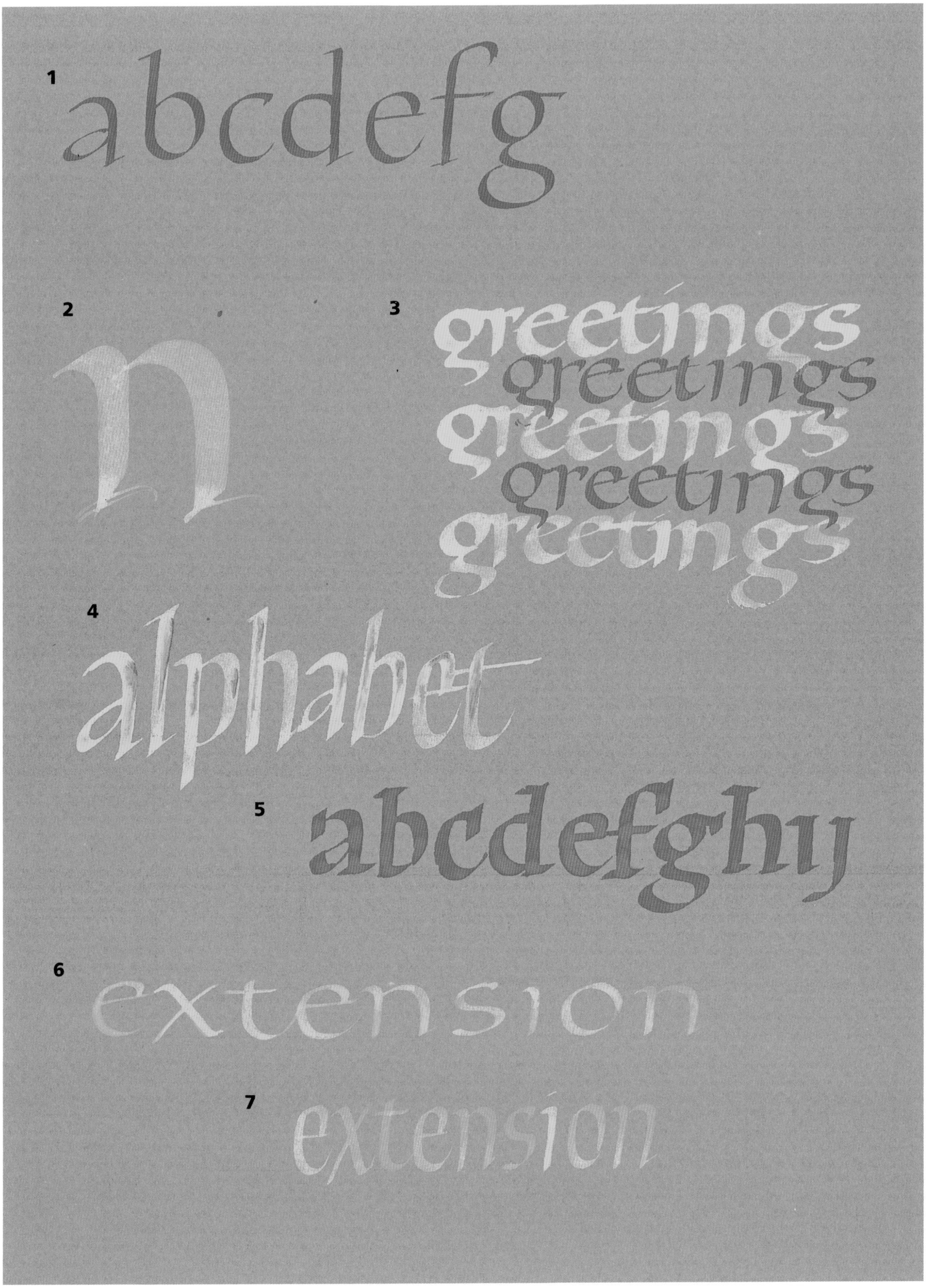

1 abcdefg

2 n

3 greetings
greetings
greetings
greetings
greetings

4 alphabet

5 abcdefghij

6 extension

7 extension

THE UNCIAL HAND

THE UNCIAL hand is a complete alphabet on its own, having no separate lower-case form. It looks rather like an alphabet that has not quite made up its mind whether to be capital (majuscule) or lower-case (minuscule). This is because of its ancestry, dating as it does from about the seventh century when many influences were at work (see pages 12-13).

NIB-WIDTHS
Usually work at four nib-widths, but you could try three and a half or even three for heavier effects. The pen angle is flatter than for most other styles, 15° or 20° from the horizontal.

There are many versions of Uncials, but this one is comfortable in pen angle and has a contemporary look. Use it for less formal work, titles, and where you want bold text. It is particularly effective in small sizes as the simple shapes remain very readable.

LETTER SHAPES
The round 'o' shape governs the form of most letters, so ensure you keep your letters wide, especially these shown which often become narrower by mistake.

LETTER HEIGHT
Some of the letters, although they are capitals, emerge slightly above or below the guidelines (body height). This is history's first sign of a developing lower-case. Keep them absolutely minimal.

LETTER SPACING
Try to even out the spaces between letters, using your eye to judge what looks balanced. The first example is clearly unbalanced, as straight shapes can be pushed more closely together than curves. The T in this form has all that space in front, so push the following letter as close as possible next to it.

The second example shows more even spreading; those letters which do not come with their own space already attached (N, I,) need your help to give them the room they need. Others need their space limiting (R, E, T). If you are uncertain if you have it right or not, view the word upside down.

COMMON MISTAKES

| 1 | 2 | 3 | 4 | 5 | 6 | 7 |

1 Over-emphasis on the top curve and a small bowl shape make this 'a' unbalanced.

2 The top of 'd' is sagging downwards; give it a lift.

3 This 'e' is too narrow.

4 Too narrow and forward sloping.

5 Both sides of the 'm' should be rounded.

6 Twist the pen to get thinner upright strokes, and put more 'bounce' into the letter!

7 Too narrow – the bowl should be more open.

LINE SPACING

The Uncial hand can be treated as a capital form and given less space between lines of writing because of the minimal protrusions above or below the lines. (But ensure you do keep the protrusions thus.) Here compare the overall density of the block of text written with different amounts of space between the lines.

Take care, especially when choosing closer line-spacing, that the gaps between words do not end up similar in size to the gaps between lines; if they do, the eye will have trouble travelling along the lines of text, and you will create 'rivers' of white space down the page.

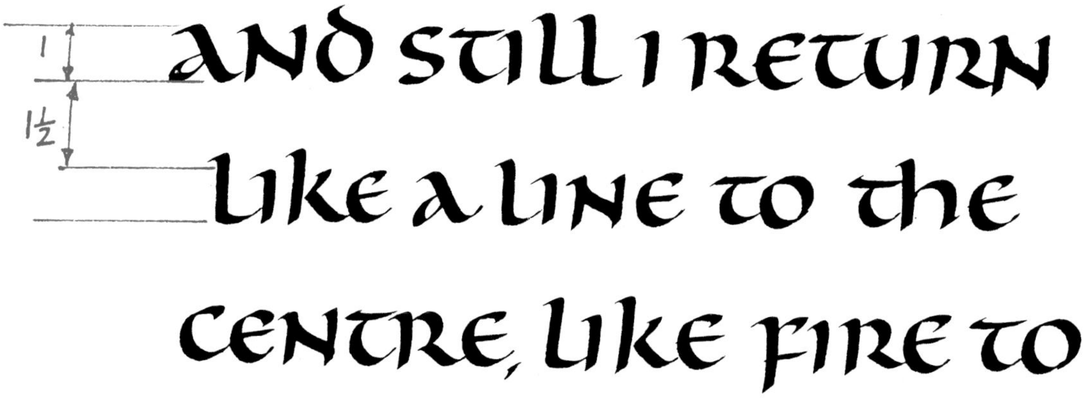

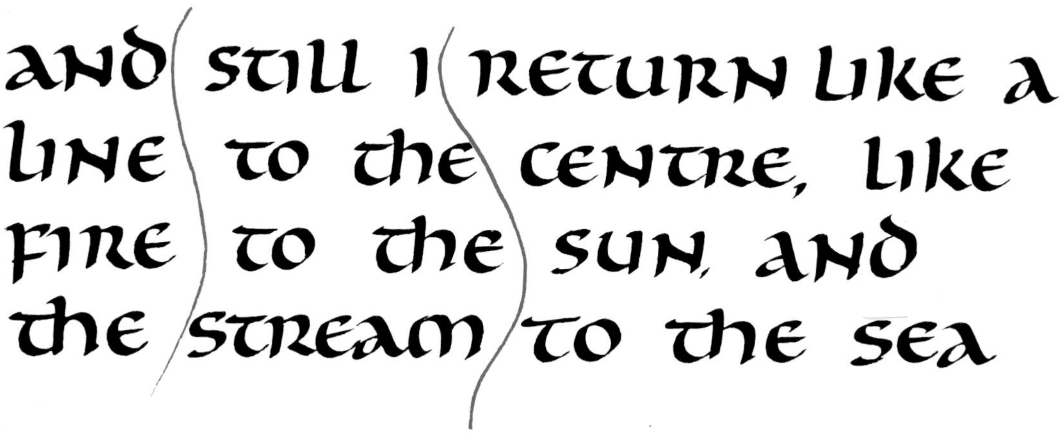

AND STILL I RETURN LIKE A LINE TO THE CENTRE, LIKE FIRE TO

AND STILL I RETURN LIKE A LINE TO THE CENTRE, LIKE FIRE TO

AND STILL I RETURN LIKE A LINE TO THE CENTRE, LIKE FIRE TO THE SUN, AND THE STREAM TO THE SEA

VARIATIONS

Opposite are some variations that you could try:

1 Flat pen angle – horizontal – with pen twists for the serifs in 'e' and 'f'.
2 Shallow and laterally spread.
3 Contrasts in weight work well in this hand because of the lack of ascenders and descenders.
4 Lightweight – about ten nib-widths.
5 Write a block of text at three or fewer nib-widths for an overall dense texture.
6 A big chunky 'a' written with an automatic pen and a colour change.
7 Lightweight, compressed, and written with speed for liveliness.
8 As in 7, but freely written with a ruling pen.

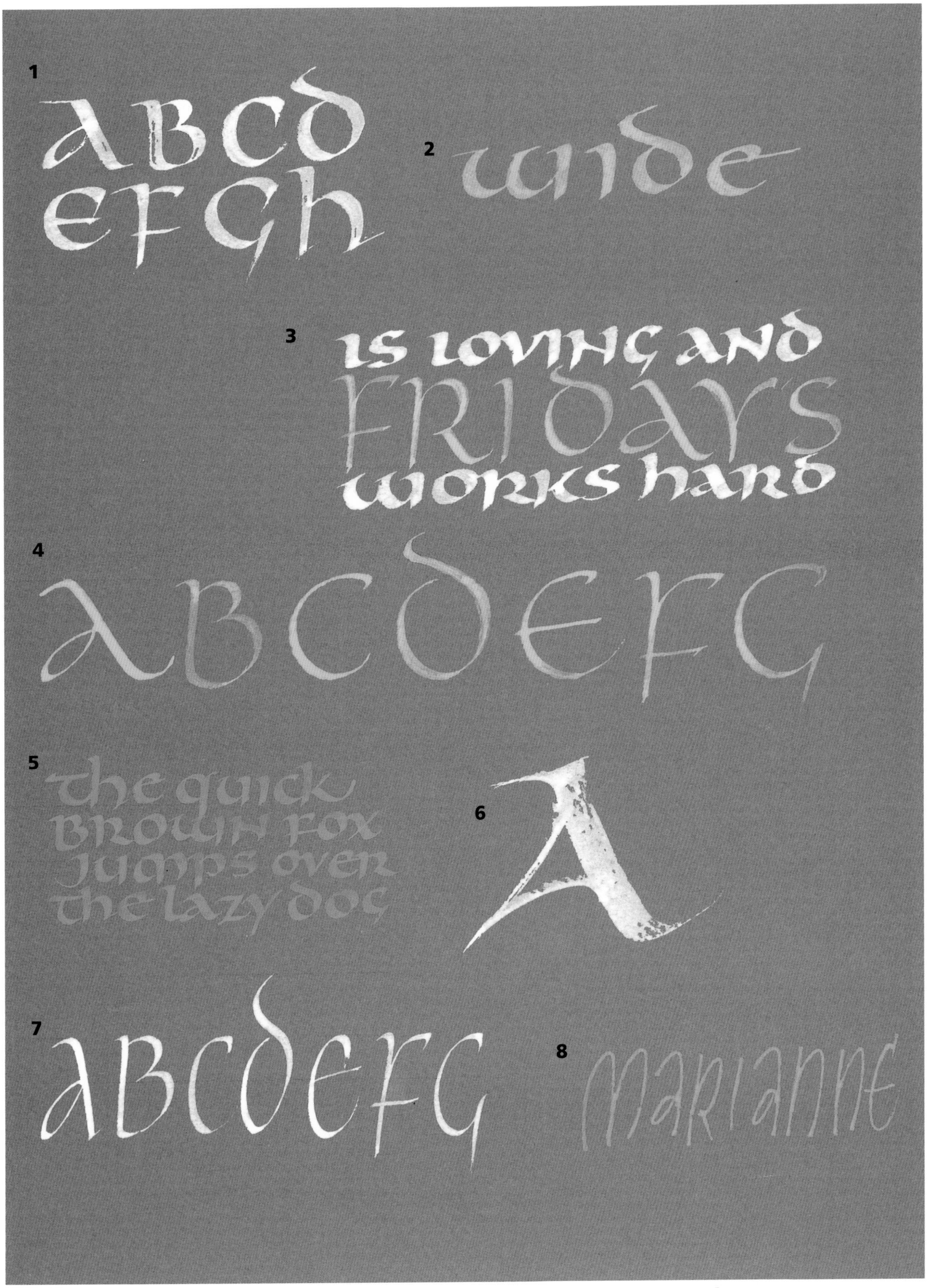

1

ABCD EFGh

2 wide

3 is loving and FRIDAYS works hard

4 ABCDEFG

5 the quick brown fox jumps over the lazy dog

6 A

7 ABCDEFG

8 marianne

GOTHIC LOWER CASE

NIB-WIDTHS

Rule lines at five nib-widths high, and never allow your ascenders or descenders to rise above or below the lines by more than two nib-widths. A pen angle of about 35° will give you the solid weight on the vertical strokes while retaining solidity on the diagonals.

THIS SOLID, vertical-stroke letterform enjoyed its heyday from the thirteenth to the sixteenth centuries. It had evolved slowly from the rounded Carolingian style which became more and more laterally compressed over time (see pages 12-13). All resemblance to its antecedent disappeared once the smooth curves gave way to angular strokes.

Variations for decorative effect included flat bottoms ('precissus'), diamonds at top and bottom ('textura') and optional extras like hairline flourishes and split tops to ascenders.

The example here is a basic version, which will serve many purposes. Take care to keep the strokes close together to retain its sturdy character. Choose it for texts requiring visual impact from its solidity and overall texture rather than instant readability.

Contemporary uses might be as single titles evoking an historic theme, certificates, prayers, or quotations from medieval times.

With it you can use Roman Capitals (page 28), Versals (page 68) or the Gothic Capitals which follow (page 44); all of these were traditionally used with this style.

LETTER SHAPES

The most important feature to retain in Gothic script is its evenness of texture. Keep all the upright strokes the same distance apart, within letters and between them, and ensure that the white which is left is no wider than the black.

Note how all the letters are based on the 'o' shape. The diagonal strokes which define the arches do not have any thin parts; they are diamonds attached to the uprights by their points.

LETTER SPACING

The first word illustrates some awkward combinations of letters. An 'r' followed by an 'a' or an 'e' followed by an 's' sets their combined gaps facing each other, resulting in more space than is desirable for an even texture. In this example the straight vertical letters have by contrast been placed too close together; compare the space inside the letter with the space either side.

Try again, cramming the 'r' and 'a' as close together as possible, likewise the 'e' and 's', and make sure all the vertical strokes maintain a regularity of distance apart.

COMMON MISTAKES

| 1 | 2 | 3 | 4 | 5 | 6 | 7 |

1 Too wide; compare the width of the white with the width of the black.

2 The arch is too thin; make a diamond not a curve.

3 The tops and feet are too horizontal.

4 The ascender is too long (unless it is on the top line).

5 The descender is too long and not compact enough.

6 Keep ascenders under two nib-widths high.

7 Divide the letter half-way.

WORD AND LINE SPACING

The space between words should be no more than the width of the letter 'o' – just sufficient to differentiate words. Wider gaps will destroy the textural quality.

This example shows the standard spacing between lines; provided the writing is kept compact, with minimal ascenders and descenders, a gap equal to the body height is sufficient, and will help to maintain the solid overall texture.

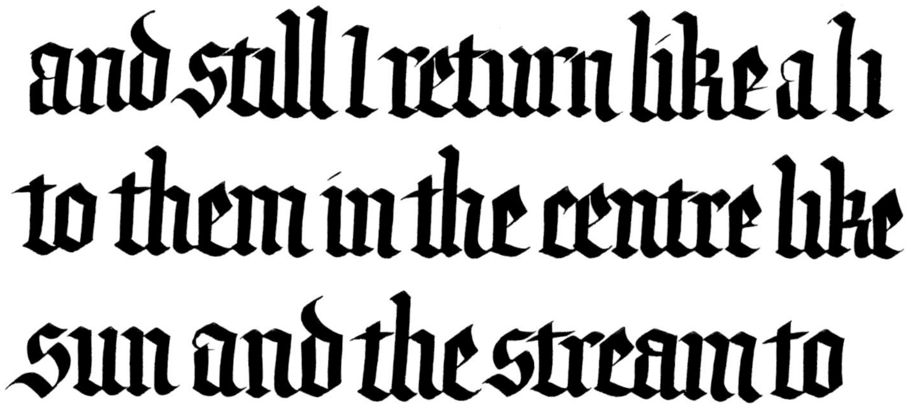

and still I return like a li to them in the centre like sun and the stream to

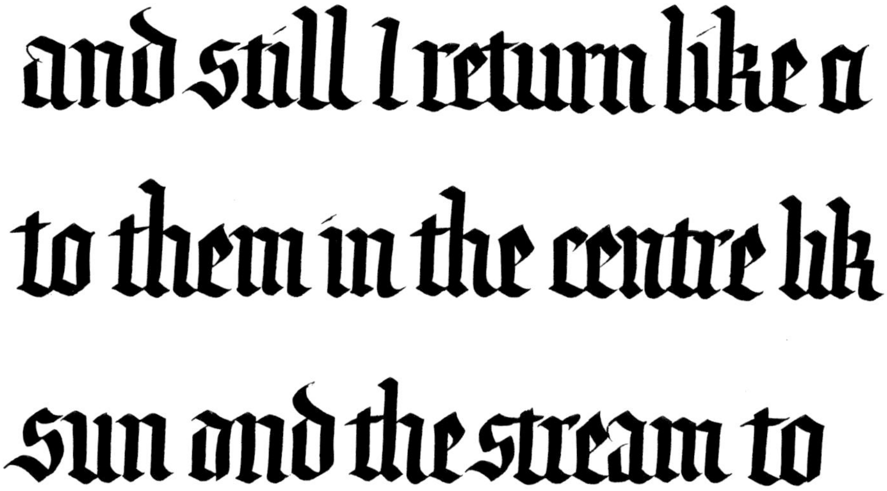

and still I return like a to them in the centre lik sun and the stream to

WIDER-SPACED

Compare the overall texture of this wider-spaced version with the first example. This much space between lines is not necessary unless the lines are very long (say, two or three times as long as here).

OPEN AND TOO CLOSE

If the writing is more open, you introduce more white into the texture; more space between the lines will be necessary. Here the ascenders and descenders are also longer than traditionally called for, and this also requires more space between the lines than has been provided here.

every person like the fire

VARIATIONS

Try some of the variations shown opposite:

1 Very tall and narrow.
2 Three nib-widths high.
3 Squat and rounded – an Italian version of Gothic.
4 Thin, with broken joins and pen twisting.
5 Five nib-widths, subtle twists.

6 Cursive Gothic, three nib-widths.
7 Lightweight with pen manipulation.
8 Using an automatic pen, manipulated, thin lines made with pen held sideways.

1

tall
and
thin

2 abcdefgh

3 rotunda

4 abcd 5 bed

6 abcdefghy

7 defghyk 8

GOTHIC CAPITALS

THESE CAPITALS are for use with the Gothic Lower Case shown on pages 40-43. Their highly decorative appearance makes them an ideal foil for the plain solidity of the lower case; they are like ornamental gates in the long fencing of lower-case text. Do not use them on their own, as a word of any length written entirely in these capitals will be very difficult to read.

NIB-WIDTHS

Write the capitals at six nib-widths high, so they are just a little higher than the body height of the lower case; you could make them up to seven nib-widths high.
The pen angle is approximately 35°, as in the lower case.

Historically capitals were not used as frequently in a block of text as we are accustomed to do today; they were employed to indicate the start of a new sentence or verse. Their relative scarcity in old manuscripts hinders comprehensive research into compiling an authentic set of letters, so these have been fabricated to form a matching set based on studies of incomplete examples (for more information on how to study manuscripts for yourself, see Be A Script Detective on page 76).

If you check other calligraphy books, you will find the greatest variety and difference will be evident in the Gothic Capitals, both for the above reason and because the Gothic period was a lengthy one and many fancy adaptations were developed in the course of time.

Another form of capital frequently used with Gothic is the Versal (see pages 68-71), usually at the start of a paragraph or verse, hence its name.

LETTER SHAPES

If you study the alphabet closely, you will see that while all the letters have distinctive features, many of them share a common basic structure. See how the letters C, E, G, O, Q and T all start with the same basic strokes.

N, M, R, P, A, B and D in this style all begin with a hook stroke and exaggerated base serif; try copying the letters in their shape groups as shown.

COMMON MISTAKES

1 Make the D wider, and execute the first stroke with more curve and energy.

2 Spread the first stroke widely, to leave more room for the parallel stroke.

3 Change the proportions, especially the relationship of the bowl of the R to the leg.

4 It is more common to break the O to the left rather than to the right, matching the other letters.

5 Set the F more upright and straighten up the drooping top curve.

fencing with Gates of capitals

DON'T

DECORATIVE CAPITALS

The capitals (above) are intended to be decorative, because they occur infrequently, and provide some visual interest in a stretch of Gothic writing – like a gate in a fence.

LETTER SPACING

Fit the capitals snugly with the lower case, as shown in these names (below), making sure there is not too much gap between the capital and the following smaller letters.

MAKE IT READABLE

These letterforms (above) were never intended for use on their own – they are too ornamental and the reader needs clues from the context of the other letters in the (lower-case) word, in order to confirm what letter it is. So a whole word or more written entirely in Gothic capitals can be too much of a good thing, making readability difficult; don't do it.

Theo Peter
May Queen

VARIATIONS

1 Lightweight, freely written.
2 Using an automatic pen, revealing the rough paper; the pen is manipulated for subtleties in the weight of strokes.
3 Traditional styling, with hairline decoration using the pen sideways.

4 Exuberant S, lightweight, pen twisting for the parallel stroke to avoid the effect being too solid.
5 Another exuberance demonstrating the varieties of S found in historic examples.

6 Letters with decorative 'thorns' and diamonds.
7 Chunky O's – about three nib-widths high.
8 Experimental double-stroke trials for variety – not yet perfected!

FORMAL ITALIC LOWER CASE

The ITALIANS developed this hand in the fifteenth century during the Renaissance. They looked at tenth-century Carolingian styles for inspiration, and developed their own version, elliptical and sloping (see pages 12-13 for an explanation of the historical background).

This is the most popular calligraphic hand today, on account of its readability, flowing quality and its adaptability for variation.

Use this form with Italic or Roman Capitals. Formal Italic suits many uses, from memorial books to poetry and expressive works.

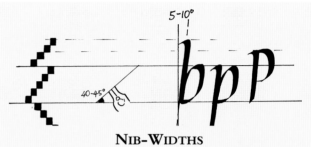

NIB-WIDTHS

Rule lines for a gap of five nib-widths, and make the ascenders and descenders just a little less than the body height, i.e. four nib-widths. The pen angle should be about 40°, and the letters slope forward by 5° to 10°.

LETTER SHAPES

See how closely related the letters above are in shape to one another; the 'a' shape is reflected in 'd', 'g', 'q', 'u', and 'y'. Turn the 'a' upside down and you have the underlying shape for 'b', 'h', 'm', 'n', 'p' and 'r'. The letters which most closely relate to the 'o' are 'e' and 'c', but you can see the affinity to the other 'a' and 'b' shapes.

CRITICAL SHAPES

The 'down-and-up' structure of 'a' (right) is a critical shape to master; it is important to take the stroke right back up to the line, and not to stop near the base as in the third example here. Try it first with a pencil; the pushing movement required may feel alien at first with the edged pen.

ARCHES

This is an exercise in arches. The first 'n' (top left) shows how to keep the pen on the page and write the whole letter in one go, but it branches out too low. Aim for the second version, where the branching arch emerges about halfway up the upright. The third example still branches, but emerges rather higher up than usually desirable. The last is not italic, and is to be avoided at all costs! It has been made without the 'branching' and by taking the pen off the paper to start anew at the top, which makes a Foundational-type arch.

COMMON MISTAKES

1   2   3   4   5   6   7   8   9

1 The pen stopped at the bottom instead of travelling right up to the top of the letter.

2 Make a corner at the top rather than a curve.

3 The ascender could be taller.

4 These arches are Foundational, not Italic; 'm' should be written without taking the pen off the page, so the arches should look 'branching' not 'stuck on'.

5 The hook at the end does not match the other letters; keep it a gentle curve.

6 Flatten the top and bottom of the 's'.

7 Flatten the bottom curve of the 'g' to avoid this stroke becoming the most dominant.

8 Divide 'e' nearer the top.

9 An uneven 'o'; this is the hardest letter to balance.

LETTER SPACING

Take care to think ahead as you write, to imagine how much space you will need between each letter as you write it. The first 'rv' are too far apart and the letters create a large inner gap – tuck them together. Double 't' and 'ft' can share a cross-bar.

The first example (right) shows uneven letter spacing; compare the space between 'z' and 'y', and between 'm' and 'e'. You should aim for an evenness between upright strokes, so spread 'm' from 'e', and tuck 'y' into 'z' to fill some of the space.

LINE SPACING

The standard gap between lines of text for Italic is double spacing, i.e. twice the body height of the text. This allows for ascenders and descenders to fit without clashing, and helps readability.

Sometimes if a closer texture is needed for your design, to give a denser overall appearance, you can write single-spaced (right). Take care with clashes, and check that you are keeping the elliptical nature of the hand; if the writing becomes too rounded, you will introduce more white into the page and you will need the extra gap between the lines to help legibility.

please close the door

On occasions when very few words are being used, they can benefit from clustering to give the overall shape greater impact to attract the eye.

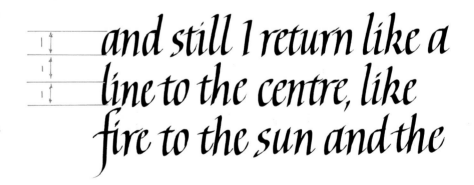

VARIATIONS

Once you have practised the letter forms, try some of the variations shown opposite:

1. Automatic pen; twisted from flat to 45°.

2. Lightweight – about ten nib-widths high.

3 Shallow and laterally spread.

4 Playing with the axis.

5 Closely packed for a solid effect.

6 An alternative style of ascender.

7 Solid writing at four nib-widths.

8 Two weights of manipulated pen writing showing changes of angle.

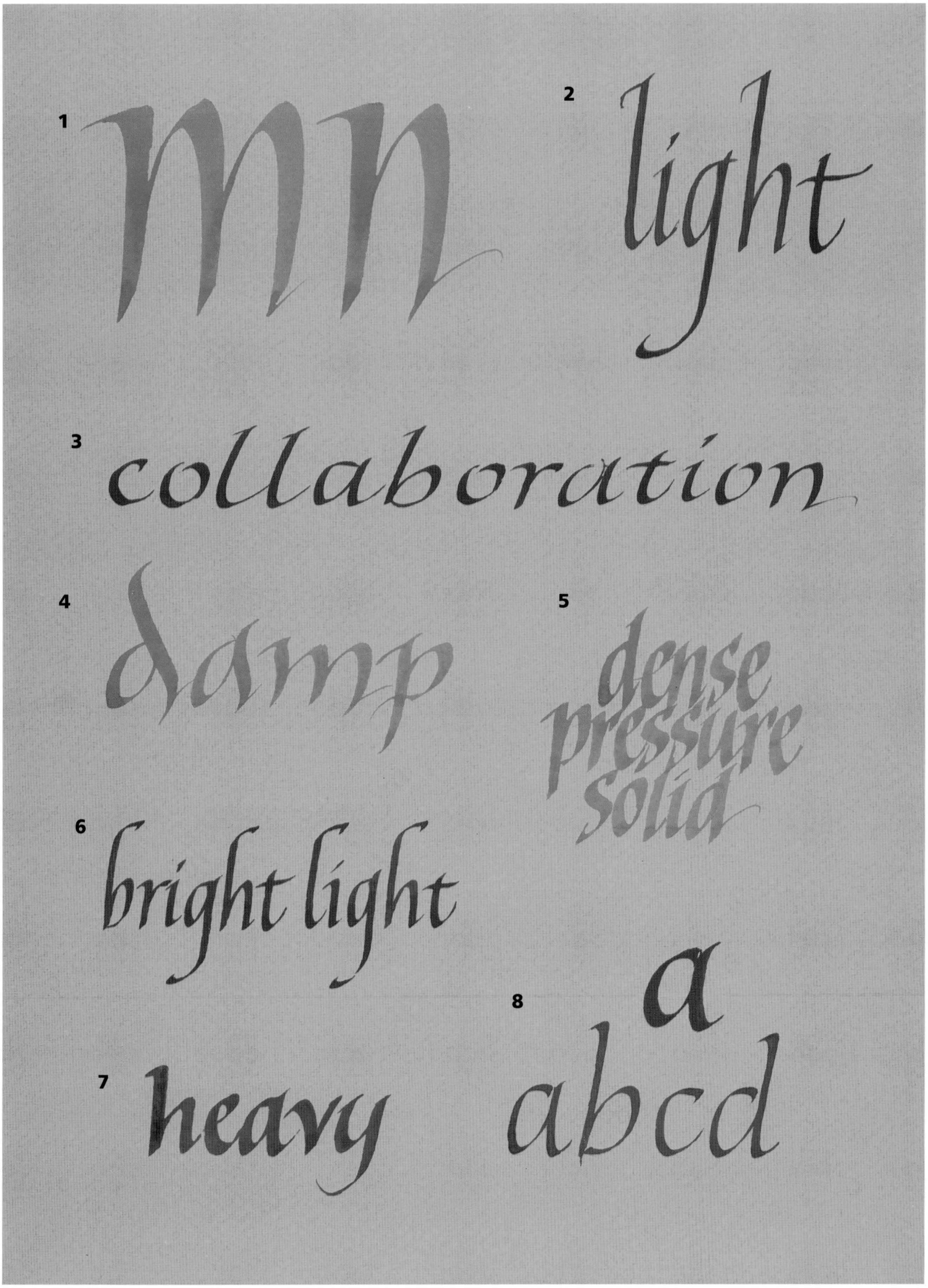

1 mn

2 light

3 collaboration

4 damp

5 dense pressure solid

6 bright light

7 heavy

8 a

abcd

ITALIC CAPITALS

ITALIC CAPITALS are based on classical Roman Capitals, but they are compressed and sloped in order to complement the lower-case Formal Italic. They evolved during the twentieth century with the revival of interest in the italic hand as a calligraphic form; previously the Italian writing masters used versions of the Roman Capitals. Your understanding of these capitals will be greater, and you will write them more easily, if you already have some knowledge of the proportions of Roman Capitals (see page 28).

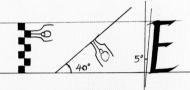

NIB-WIDTHS

Seven nib-widths are commonly used, although eight will provide slightly more slender and elegant versions. The pen angle varies occasionally, but on average it is 40° from the horizontal.

The letters have a slight slope, usually about 5° from the vertical, but it is acceptable to have a steeper slope (but don't vary the slope in one piece of work!). The effect of 40° plus the slope means that the horizontal strokes are thinner than the vertical ones, which produces a subtler effect than if all strokes were the same thickness.

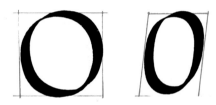 

ROMAN COMPARISONS

Compare the Roman letter O with the Italic form, and you will see what a difference compression and slope makes. The Italic version is approximately one-third narrower than the Roman. Roman Capital letters conform to several width groups (see pages 28-29); with compression, the difference between the Italic groups is less obvious, and both the wide group (such as O) and the three-quarter group (such as N) occupy the same width. Half-width letters become just a bit narrower than the others.

FITTING CAPITALS WITH LOWER CASE

If you are writing mainly in lower case, then only rule lines for the lower-case letters (see below), and use your eye to judge the capital height. The ascenders of the lower case letters should extend higher than the capital itself.

'UPLIFT'

When you write with a slope in Italic Capitals, take note of what you are doing with the horizontal strokes. They should stay parallel to the writing line, or they may be slightly raised. If they point downwards, they give your letters a depressed look. Go for uplift! Even the curved letters, like B and D, can be given slight uplift on their top curves.

COMMON MISTAKES

B E M S R A H

1   2   3   4   5   6   7

1 Make the join of the B higher up.

2 This E is too wide at the top and bottom, and it would be improved by a serif at the top left.

3 M is unbalanced; look at the shapes created between the two uprights.

4 The S is top-heavy; look at it upside-down – much better!

5 R's leg is set too low down and is too heavy.

6 The cross-bar on A could be lower.

7 Put serifs on the H to give it subtlety.

WHEN WE TRY TO PICK

OUT ANYTHING BY ITS

WE FIND IT HITCHED

WHEN WE TRY TO PICK

OUT ANYTHING BY ITS

ELF WE FIND IT HITCH

WRITING ALL IN CAPITALS

When you are writing a whole line or more in capitals, it is essential to establish a top line to stop heights drifting. For a block of text like this (above) written all in capitals, you can experiment with the inter-line spacing. First try its own height as the space; this gives plenty of room for the eye to follow the line, even a very long one, without confusion. For a denser effect, it is better if the lines are not too long; try an inter-line space of half the line height.

WHEN WE TRY TO
PICK OUT ANYTH
BY ITSELF WE FIND

LIGHTWEIGHT, TEXTURAL

If you are more interested in a textural effect and not so much in the readability, try writing with no inter-line spaces. In this example above, a lighter weight (more nib-widths) has been used.

VARIATIONS

Italic capitals lend themselves to playful variety; here are some examples shown opposite.

1 Heavy weight – about five nib-widths high.

2 Tall and narrow – a block of text with no interline space can be effective.

3 Manipulated pen – difficult at first, you twist the pen as you move down the stroke.

4 Written at speed, and with the pen well-loaded with ink.

5 More pen manipulation, this time twisting several ways.

6 Double stroke; the second thinner stroke is made with the pen held sideways in a flicking motion.

7 Pointed, with exaggerated serifs, written at speed.

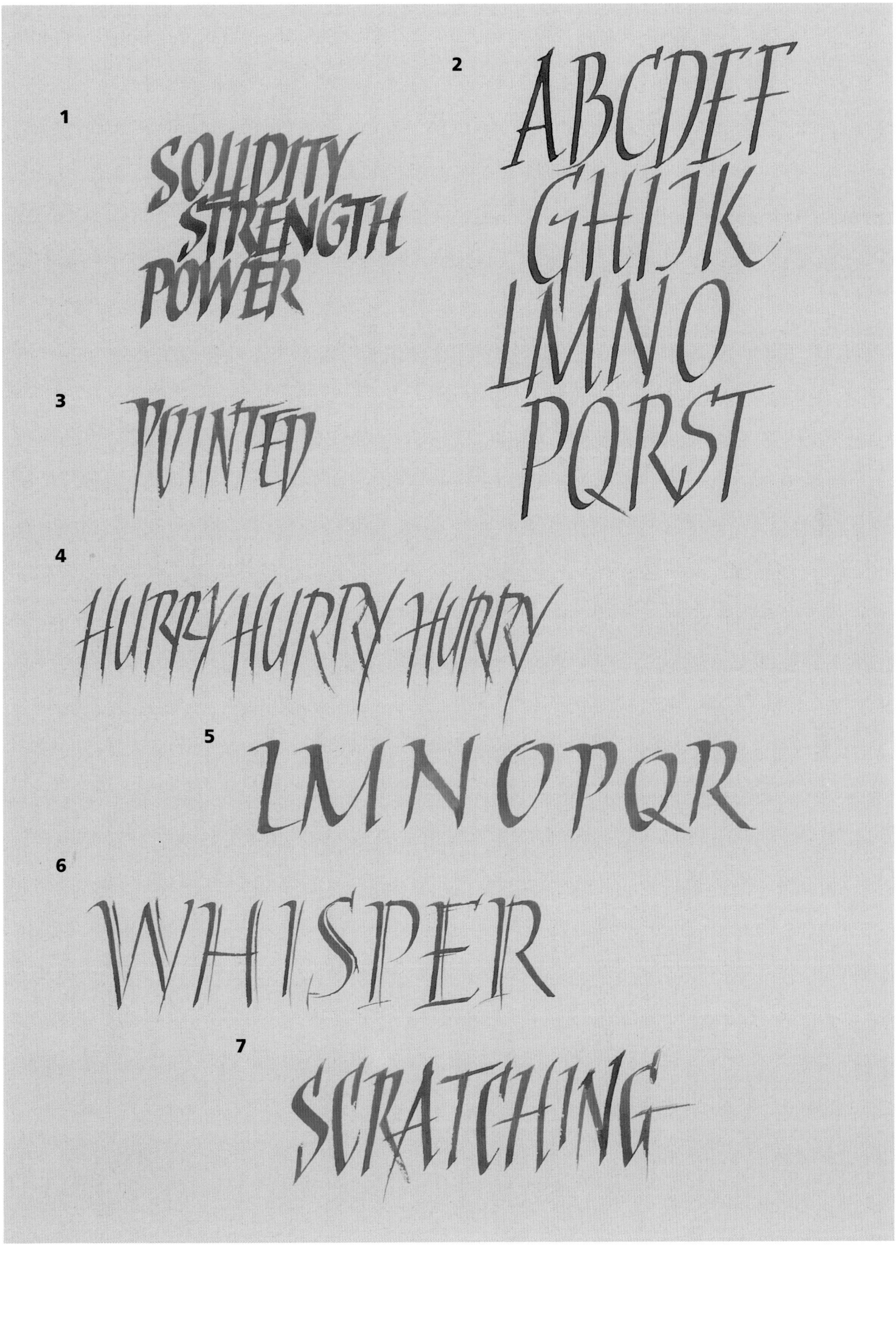

1

SOLIDITY
STRENGTH
POWER

2

ABCDEF
GHIJK
LMNO
PQRST

3

POINTED

4

HURRY HURRY HURRY

5

LMNOPQR

6

WHISPER

7

SCRATCHING

POINTED ITALIC

THIS IS a lively contemporary hand, which lends itself to many variations. You will understand this style better if you first become familiar with the Formal Italic. When you first try it, the sharp pointed nature of the letters may feel alien to you, but do persevere as it has many exciting possibilities as a modern Italic style – imagine using it for a poem about frosty weather, for example. It should be written fairly quickly, with sharp changes of direction instead of the gentle curves of the Formal version.

NIB-WIDTHS
Write at five nib-widths high for your line spacing, and at a 45° pen angle. The letters slope forward slightly (about 5-10°).

LETTER SHAPES
The 'a' bowl shape governs many others in this alphabet. Now view it upside-down to see how 'b' and other letters would be formed in a similar way.

The sharp arch of the 'n' also governs many arched letters.

AWKWARD COMBINATIONS:
Join the crossbars in 'ft'; keep the top of the 'f' narrow when an 'l' follows it; tuck letters into one another if otherwise they will cause spacing irregularities.

LETTERSPACING
Aim for an even rhythm of upright strokes. While this is straightforward when writing parallel letters ('u', 't', 'i'), a shape such as 'v' needs to have adjacent letters tucked in close to it.

COMMON MISTAKES

1. Keep both upright strokes of the 'a' parallel.
2. The arch in 'b' should branch out in one movement from the stem stroke.
3. The diagonal stroke in 'z' needs to be heavier – flatten your pen angle.
4. Is this 'u' or 'n'? Take care with branching arches.
5. Put a top on the 's'.
6. The cross-bar of the 't' is too thick, meaning that the pen angle is too steep.
7. This 'y' is too wide, creating a thick first stroke.

WORD SPACING AND LINE SPACING

For most italic forms the standard spacing between lines is twice the body height of the letter. However, this can look too generous sometimes with Pointed Italic when it is a little narrower than its Formal counterpart, and a narrower gap between lines may look more suitable.

1 The standard gap between lines is twice the body height of the letters.

2 A narrower gap between the lines has been used here. This is particularly effective if the lines are not very long, and the ascenders and descenders are adjusted so as not to clash.

1

and where 'tis fine it sends
some precious instance of
itself after the thing it loves

2

and where 'tis fine it sends
some precious instance of
itself after the thing it loves

3

and (where) 'tis fine it
sends) some (precious inst
itself) after (the thing it

3 If you choose a narrower gap between lines, take care to avoid big spaces between words, as these can become as wide as the line spacing and create unsightly 'rivers' of white down the page.

4

some precious
itself after
thinks on

4 Over-generous ascenders and descenders have caused a tangled overlap of letters which affects legibility.

VARIATIONS

Try copying some of these examples shown on the opposite page.

1 Low arches, written rapidly.
2 Lightweight, narrow, and written quickly.
3 Lightweight and even narrower, with curved, wispy ascenders.
4 Lightweight and very wide.
5 Standard nib-widths, but very narrow.
6 Narrow, lightweight and joined up.
7 Standard version but joined up.
8 Changes of slope, with 'dancing' movement.
9 Lightweight, narrow, written slowly.

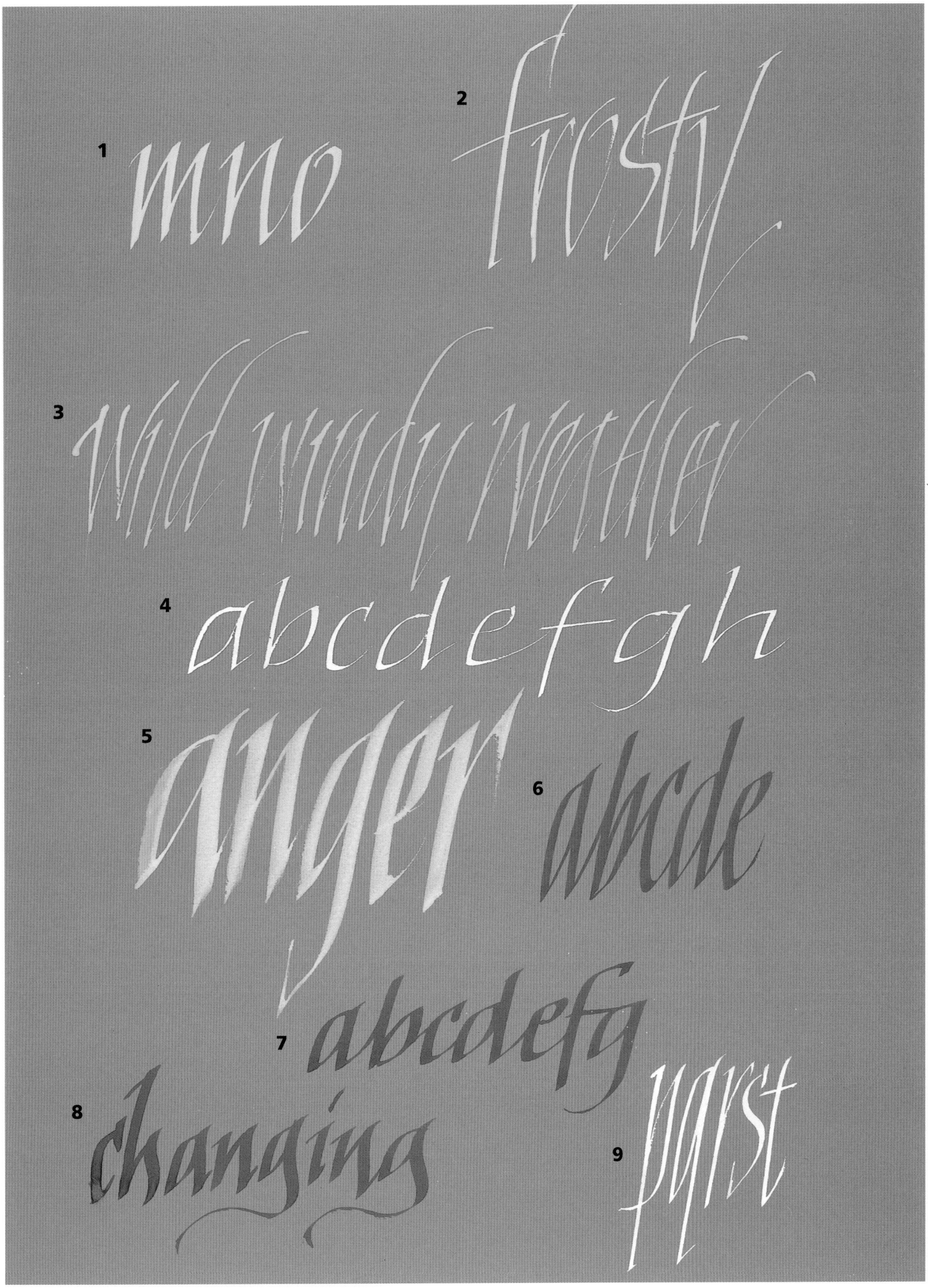

1 mno

2 frosty

3 wild windy weather

4 abcdefgh

5 anger

6 abcde

7 abcdefg

8 changing

9 pqrst

FLOURISHED ITALIC

FLOURISHING IS fun to do, and there are many variations to try. While other letterforms can be ornamented by a few extension strokes, it is the Italic form which lends itself to elaborate and boisterous enhancement. The Italian writing masters of the sixteenth century established the practice, at a time of high unemployment for scribes when their trade was being supplanted by the printing press. These writing masters harnessed the printed page as a means of distributing teaching manuals, in which they showed off their skills in elaborate flourishing and beautiful writing.

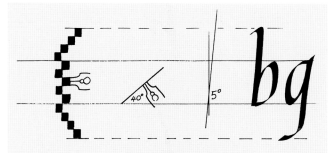

NIB-WIDTHS

As with Formal Italic, rule lines at five nib-widths high, but allow more space above and below for ascenders and descenders. The pen angle is 40°, but with some twisting for the more complex flourishes.

LINE ENDINGS

In a block of text, it is sometimes useful to be able to make an extension stroke from the last letter to fill up a short line; not all letters will oblige, but here are some effective examples below. Aim to keep the extension either horizontal or rising, try to avoid a droopy one.

FIRST ATTEMPTS

When you first try flourishes, keep them simple. Make them just a little taller than usual, with a simple hook serif. Take care to keep the main part of the stroke straight; do not anticipate the curve too soon or you will make a weak, bendy mark. As your confidence grows, try taller ones, then wider, then a stroke curved back on itself. This last must only be attempted when there is plenty of clearance, as flourishes too close to the body of the letter can look crowded.

COMMON MISTAKES

1 The flourish is too close to the body of the letter; it needs to be more generous.

2 The end of this ascender looks droopy.

3 Try to avoid making a descender the thickest stroke in the letter.

4 Sagging extension to 'r' – it needs uplift.

5 The descender of the 'y' and the ascender of the 'h' have anticipated the curve too soon, making them too weak.

6 Not enough clearance between the flourish and the body of the letter.

FLOURISHING WITHIN A BLOCK OF TEXT

When you want to write several lines of text, it is usually best to keep any flourishes within the main text relatively modest, and, if need be, go to town with those along the top and bottom line, where there is plenty of room (only attempt this if there is plenty of room, of course).

all all all

DOUBLE ASCENDERS

What should you do when two ascenders come together? Here are some possibilities; the safest answer is to keep the first one plain and go wild with the second one. Above are three versions to try.

all singing and shining together as one, the whole universe appears as an infinite storm of beauty

all singing and shining

all singing and shining

all singing and shining

USING FREER TOOLS

The making of flourishes needs expansive movements, and we use a tool which sometimes resists such expansiveness. This has encouraged calligraphers to search for a pen which allows freer movement. As a result the humble ruling pen has been rescued from its humdrum existence as a technical instrument for making thin lines, and become the architect of our liberation. Here are three examples of ruling-pen writing, which enhance the possibilities of flourishing.

VARIATIONS

Try copying some of these examples shown on the opposite page.

1 Some wilder flourishes, easier with a smaller nib and plenty of ink.
2 The bowl of the 'p' is formed in one movement, curving right round at the bottom and extending out past the upright stem.
3 Double flourishes take some designing; this one uses a thinner nib for the second flourish.
4 Heavier weight, pointed letters, on a rougher paper surface giving a texture to the strokes.
5 One word, three flourishes!
6 Heavy weight, narrow, pointed, speedily written
7 Try some flourishes without letters – they fill small gaps at the end of pages.

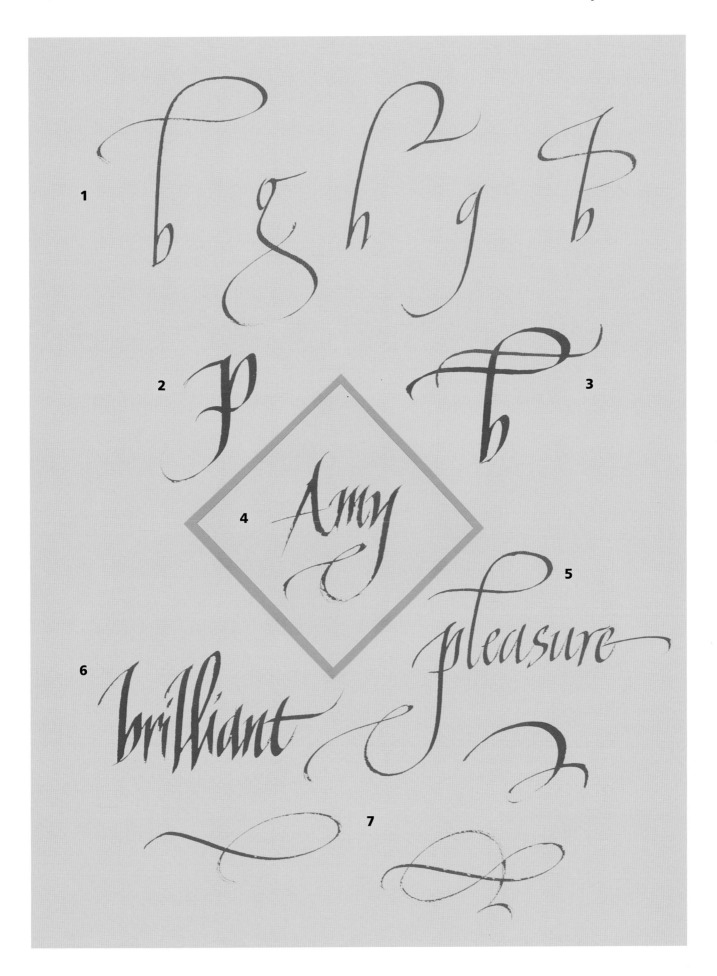

FLOURISHED ITALIC CAPITALS

FLOURISHING IS one of the greatest delights in calligraphy, both in the performance and in the beholding. To make good shapes, you need confident motion – only practice will give you this – and a sound knowledge of the underlying basic form, which is the Italic Capital (see page 52). Flourished letters take up a lot more space than do their formal counterparts, so don't even think about flourishing if your space is limited. Keep your pen well loaded with ink: this lubricates the movement and aids the flow, which has to be steady but fairly quick. You can use these with Formal Italic Lower Case (page 48) or with the flourished version (page 60).

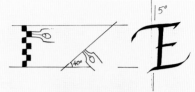

NIB-WIDTHS
Rule lines at seven nib-widths, and hold the pen at approximately 40° from the horizontal. The letters slope 5° or more. As with the Italic Capitals, make sure your horizontal strokes, such as in the E, have slight 'uplift' rather than any hint of a downward leaning.

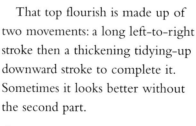

THE TOP FLOURISH
It is no accident that the flowing parts of most of these flourished letters extend to the left of the letter; this assumes there will be more text to follow, and allows room for it.

That top flourish is made up of two movements: a long left-to-right stroke then a thickening tidying-up downward stroke to complete it. Sometimes it looks better without the second part.

FITTING TOGETHER
Consider monograms: when two letters are to be fitted together in a design, you must experiment with variants on flourishes to find ways of keeping the extensions to the outside and allowing the area where they meet to mesh together.

AVOIDING GAPS
With the flourish positioned at the start of the R, the rest of the name 'Rachel' can follow without any worrying gaps. Problems arise when a more ambitious end stroke pushes away for some distance the letters that complete the word!

COMMON MISTAKES

1 2 3 4 5 6

1 The first stroke is too weak and needs to reach the base line.

2 This flourish is droopy – make it more horizontal.

3 The underlying H is obscured by the wild curve of the first stroke.

4 The M has sprawled too far and is losing its underlying form.

5 The drooping top makes a confusion with a J a possibility.

6 More drooping! This flourish looks like an afterthought.

MENU

Flourished capitals do not work well together in any great number, as their individual flamboyances can lead to a very busy design. If you want to write a title in flourished capitals, then minimize the extensions within the word, and confine the flamboyance to the first and last characters.

MENU

MENU

Maryline

M M M

Mary

VARIATIONS FOR 'M'

Here is a typical example with simple flourished lower case; if the ascenders and descenders are kept fairly plain, you can play with the possibilities for the capital – complex flourishing in the capital will rarely work with equally boisterous flourished ascenders and descenders.

Here are some variations on an M to set you thinking; try them out and then experiment with other letters.

The fancier the decoration in the initial, the plainer you can afford to make the 'y', as here in 'Mary'.

VARIATIONS

Try copying some of these examples shown on the opposite page.

1 Written with speed, and a double stroke.
2 Incorporating an ascender.
3 Freely written, lightweight (about ten nib-widths). This needs plenty of ink to keep the strokes free-flowing.
4 Very elaborate flourishes need a light touch, speed, and a fully-charged nib.
5 Diamonds have been inserted after the letter is made; this is done by interrupting the stroke when it is first made.
6 Written with speed.
7 Heavyweight (five nib-widths) with minimal flourishes; gold paint has been added in the spaces when the ink is dry.
8 Written very quickly with a ruling pen.
9 Lightweight lettering – the large flourish contrasts strongly with the pointed italic name.
10 Wider, freely styled, overwritten with gold paint.

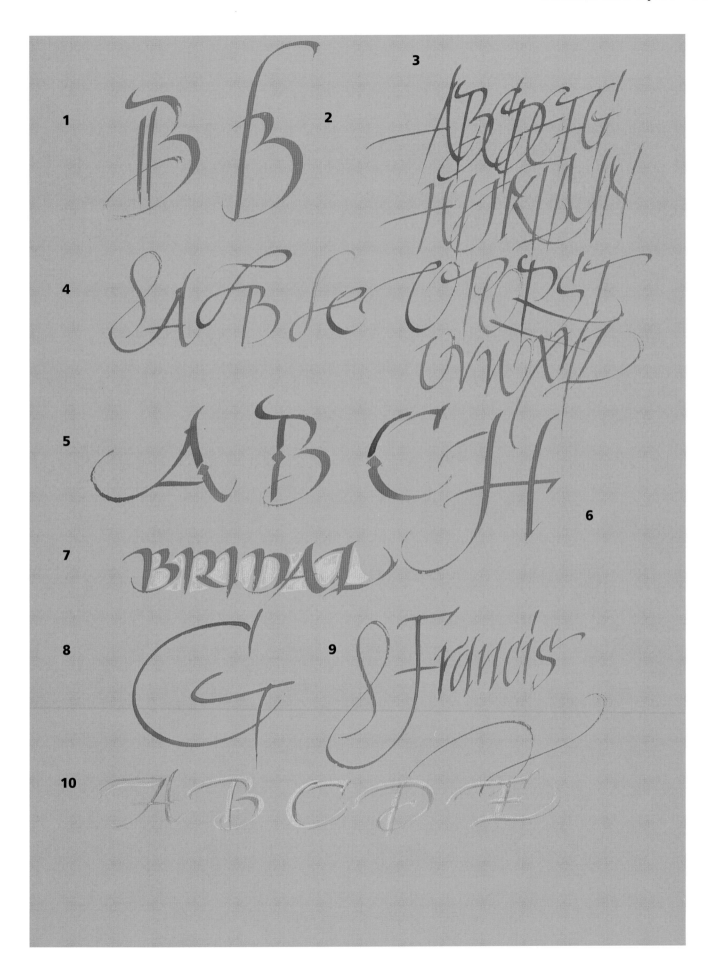

VERSALS

THE UNDERLYING forms of Versal letters are based on the classical Roman Capital (look at pages 28-29 before you begin). Originally in early manuscripts these Roman Capitals were freely drawn with a pen and used as display headings or as single letters introducing verses and paragraphs. Often freely drawn Uncial capitals were used in the same way.

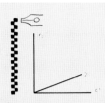

NIB-WIDTHS
The height of the Versal letter is eight times the width of the letter stem which will be the same as 24 nib-widths high.

PEN ANGLE
To draw the stem of the letters, the edge of the nib is held at 0° angle (i.e. straight) producing the widest line for the down-stroke of each letter and the fine horizontal serifs at the top and bottom.

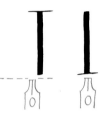

CROSS-STROKES
To draw the cross-strokes of letters such as A, E, F, H, L and T, the pen nib is held vertically to the line. Maintain the pen vertically finally to add the serifs. This will produce a fine line.

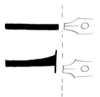

CURVES AND DIAGONALS
To enable you to draw the curves, the pen should be held at a slight angle (about 20°) and held at the best angle to make the widest line for diagonals.

PROPORTIONS
Versal letters are based on the proportions of Roman Capitals (see pages 28-29), therefore the form of O is circular with an inside oval shape. Draw the oval shape first with the pen, then add the weight to the outside circle.

LETTER STROKES
Each Versal letter is made of compound strokes. Each letter stem is drawn with two outer strokes, slightly waisted to create elegance, and a third stroke in the middle to fill the letter with ink, so completing it. Each letter stem should be three nib-widths at its widest point otherwise it becomes too heavy.

ADAPTATION
The Versal letter is normally written upright in keeping with its classical Roman origins. However, contemporary Versals can be adapted to use in different ways. A simple change from upright to a slant means that they can be used with Italic. They can be compressed, stretched and weighted (made to look heavy).

These elegant letters will become easier once you have become familiar with the pen angle changes and the sequence of how to build up each letter. It may be helpful to draw the skeleton letter shapes with a pencil as a guide.

COMMON MISTAKES

| 1 | 2 | 3 | 4 | 5 | 6 | 7 | 8 |

1 A is not upright; the inside apex should be central. The strokes of A should overlap at the top.

2 The middle cross-bar should equal the length of the top cross-bar.

3 The stem is too waisted and rather heavy.

4 The serif is too thick; keep it smaller.

5 Do not splay the legs of M; it becomes too wide as a result.

6 Keep the inside shape in O oval; keep the letter rounded at the base.

7 Do not make the bowl of R too wide.

8 Keep the second down-stroke straight.

SPACING LINES, WORDS AND LETTERS

Versal Capitals should be lightweight and look freely written in character. Allow plenty of space around the letters. The oval inside shapes of O, C, D, G and Q should be reflected visually in the space left between the letters to create an open texture. Experiment with the interlinear space (space between the lines).

The interlinear space (above) is the same as the letter height giving an open look to the writing. This spacing is suitable for long lines of text, making it easier to read.

Closer interlinear spacing produces a textural feel to the writing (left). It is not so legible for long lines, but used with short lines of text it creates exciting and interesting work.

The interlinear space between the lines (right) is about half the letter height which is a comfortable standard. As a guide, to retain evenness and legibility in lines of text, the interlinear space should appear slightly larger than the space between the letters.

LETTER SPACING

FIL – the spacing between these letters is too close.
LL – spacing about right.
ED – spacing too close.
Turn your work upside down to view spacing if you find it difficult to understand – mistakes will be easier to see this way round.

MOR – fractionally more space between these letters is needed.
NIN – letters look too close; compare with 'MORNING' above.
NG – spacing between the letters should balance with the inside of the letters.

VARIATIONS

In early manuscripts display headings and initials were done in capitals using a pen. They were made with compound strokes and often coloured, usually red or blue. These Versals, as they have been called, are considered to be one of the roots of manuscript illumination. The letters on the opposite page are coloured Versals and have been constructed in the same way as the Versal alphabet shown on page 69. By adding colour and using two pens, many variations can be achieved.

NUMBERS

ROMAN NUMERALS were in common usage in Europe until at least the fifteenth century, and are still used occasionally when writing classical works. The Arabic figures that we now use took many centuries to be accepted, as the Roman heritage was very strong.

The first evidence of their arrival in Europe occurs in eleventh century. When the system finally took hold in Europe, it was found to be a much more efficient concept of counting and notation, yet Britain did not adopt Arabic numerals until the seventeenth century. We are today experiencing a similar conflict with regard to units of measurement, resulting in parallel usage of the Imperial (yes, still a Roman heritage) and metric systems.

The script style in which you are writing generally determines the weight, pen angle and slope of any numbers used, but there are some general principles to apply. The basic upright, capital-height version can be taken as the standard model that would be acceptable in use with any script. The other versions are optional extras.

NIB-WIDTHS
The basic model is written at a 30° pen angle and, if written with Roman Capitals, it matches their height of seven nib-widths. In contrast, the up-and-down version also shown is another popular device, generally designed to accompany lower-case lettering, as the effect is of having ascenders and descenders.

£45 £45

$45 $45

OTHER CHARACTERS
The $ or £ signs count as capitals, and you will find if you examine price lists in printed catalogues that the full-height version fits most needs – which caught your eye in these examples first?

AD 1254

THIS IS THE STANDARD USAGE
The numbers are the same height as the capitals.

3 cups flour

THE 'LOWER-CASE' OPTION
When these numbers are used with minuscules, they generally look comfortable together because of their appearance of having ascenders and descenders. But it is just as correct to use numerals which ascend to capital height with these letters.

Telephone 1705 3767

Tel. 1705 276432

COMBINING NUMBERS WITH ITALIC
Experiment to decide whether the numbers you want to use look best at their full height or in the 'lower-case' version. Note that here they are sloped and compressed to match the Italic style.

EXEMPLAR

A Standard version, usually used to match capital height.

B This version is frequently favoured when combined with lower-case text.

C Italic form; sloped and compressed. You could slope and compress the above version also.

A

B

1 2 3 4 5
6 7 8 9 0

C

1 2 3 4 5
6 7 8 9 0

COMMON MISTAKES

2 4 5 6 6 8 9

1   **2**   **3**   **4**   **5**   **6**   **7**

1 Keep the top in line with the base.

2 Beware of making the cross-bar too low.

3 Out of proportion – move the bowl lower.

4 The top fades out to nothing.

5 The bowl is rather small.

6 This 8 is top-heavy – look at it upside-down to confirm this.

7 The bottom tails off with a weak ending.

USING NUMBERS

Try this exercise to practise your number skills. Rule rectangles in pencil to your own choice of size, making six rows across and seven down. Then go back and add a height line, unless you feel brave enough to try this as a discipline in gauging the correct height by eye.

Before you write in pen, lightly pencil in the numbers so that if later you are distracted, you will not inadvertently miss one.

The example shown here uses the up-and-down version of the numerals to show how it looks *en masse*; for your first attempt you may prefer to use the capital-height version.

S		6	13	20	27
M		7	14	21	28
T	1	8	15	22	29
W	2	9	16	23	30
T	3	10	17	24	31
F	4	11	18	25	
S	5	12	19	26	

8-10 potatoes

½ tablespoon butter

1½ cups (350ml) milk

1 teaspoon salt

¼ teaspoon pepper

FRACTIONS

Quite a lot of numbers can occur when writing out a recipe, and here we meet fractions for the first time! If you write fractions with the cross-bar as a diagonal slash, you will find the stroke is thinner, and there is more room to write the number larger than if you had written it horizontally.

(Note for cooks – this is a Swedish recipe for creamed potatoes – peel and dice the potatoes, simmer in the milk until soft, add seasoning.)

VARIATIONS

When you are comfortable with the standard versions, try some of these variations to complement your text.

1 Lightweight, freeform.
2 Compressed, pointed.
3 Very light, more controlled than **1**.
4 A Gothic suggestion; Roman numerals would have been used at the time so we have no authentic Gothic Arabic, so to speak.
5 Flat pen angle, very rounded; might suit Uncial.
6 Solid wedges, for a heavy effect.
7 Fast, free writing with a ruling pen.

BE A SCRIPT DETECTIVE

CALLIGRAPHERS SOMETIMES want to reproduce a script they have not used before, and which is not in their calligraphy books. Perhaps you need to write names in a memorial book to match the previous scribe's style. Or you see a style you like in an advertisement or another calligrapher's work. If you know how to analyse it, you can work out how to produce a complete alphabet from a small example.

Analysis is a valuable skill to develop. Calligraphers who provide alphabet exemplars generally use it to research into photographs of historic manuscripts to check the authenticity of particular details. When you become familiar with a few scripts, you may feel that you want to do the same, and to make your own decisions. The skills of analysis will help. Here is how to sift through the clues.

Find as much as you can of the script you want to study; it is unlikely that you will find every letter if you only have a few lines to work with, but even that much will suffice, with detective work. If the sample you have is only a few millimetres high, get it enlarged on a photocopier. Whatever the size, if you do not want to deface the sample you have, take a copy to work on.

The pen nib tried indicates a weight of four nib-widths; try it yourself to see if you agree.

Rule some lines and copy an 'o' – it is oval and slightly forward-sloping, perhaps made in one sweep? Then try some other o-shaped letters. If you have experience of several alphabets, you may notice that this seems to have some Uncial letterforms but Italic arches.

Make a note of the relative length of ascenders and descenders – about two-thirds the body height? Copy a few examples.

Look at the arch formation; slightly italic, but emerging high up; this indicates a pen twist to get that thin part emerging from a smooth curve. Try 'm', 'n', 'h' and other similar shapes.

Speed: fairly swift, especially the upward flicks on 'g' and 'o'.

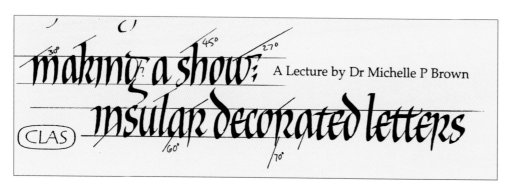

Try analysing the script on this invitation slip; here a photocopy has been made for experimentation purposes, so that the original does not have to be defaced.

Rule top and bottom lines – they are close together, but that is because they are part of a title; there would be some problems with clashing if this space was used all the time. Mark the angles at some entry and exit strokes – they vary a lot, and there seems to be some pen twisting going on to achieve the thin bottom of the 'r', and the thin arches on 'm' and 'n'.

Time to assemble all the letters we have; leave a mark to indicate any missing ones.

bb ff
pp qq
vv xx
yy zz

The 'f' presents a quandary; there are some Uncial-type letter shapes ('d', 'g' and 'r') so perhaps the 'f' should follow suit. If you were unaware of the Uncial connection though, an italic form might occur to you, but with a pointed base like 'r', and a top like 'e'. Continue this way to create the rest of the alphabet. This method will work with any script, modern or historical. Close observation is the most important factor; if there are several examples of any letter but they all differ, select the one you consider to be the best. Experience will help you develop an eye for this.

Based on the information you already have, try making up the missing letters. Should 'b' have a curved base? This might fit best with other curved letters.

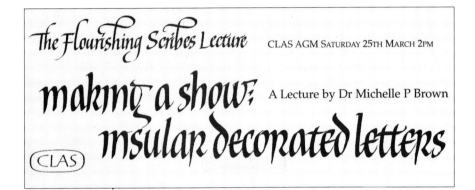

The Flourishing Scribes Lecture   CLAS AGM SATURDAY 25TH MARCH 2PM

making a show: A Lecture by Dr Michelle P Brown
insular decorated letters

(CLAS)

FOLLOW THIS EIGHT-STAGE PLAN:

1 Rule in the lines accurately at the top and bottom of the 'x' height (body height). The first thing you can find out is how much space there is between body heights – often double, sometimes only one or one and a half, occasionally three times the body height. Note this down. This is called the 'interline space'.

2 Now try to decide what pen angle has been used; obtain an average measurement by marking lines with a ruler along several of the entry and exit strokes. Then use a protractor to read off a measurement in degrees.

3 Boldness/lightness: if it looks bold, there will be a small number of 'nib-widths', if it looks lightweight, there will be more. To find out, go through your pens and find one that matches in size – hold it over a thick stroke, perhaps in an 's', at the correct pen angle, then move it round the letter to see if seems the right size. Try another if it's too small. When you are sure, put some ink in the pen and make some nib-width markings between the lines. Note down how many there are.

4 Now you know enough to rule a few lines of your own and start copying – so next look at the shapes of the letters. Look especially at the shape of the O; this is important, because O usually governs the shape of several other letters. Is it rounded, oval, upright or sloped? Compare the O with other O-shaped letters

to see how they match; try copying a few.

5 Extensions: if it is lower-case text, how tall are the ascenders and descenders in proportion to the body height – the same again, half as much again, taller? (Take an average, remember the writer did not know his work was going to be studied so closely!)

6 Arches: in lower-case letters, the joining point, for example in the letter 'h', will usually be at the top (as in Foundational) or branching out from the bottom in a joined-up movement (as in Italic). The arch shape is often a critical pointer to the main characteristics of the script.

7 Speed: you will be slow when you first try copying it, but speed is important to note, as it does affect the appearance of letters. Clues to fast writing are: slope, shorter number of strokes per letter, no fancy serifs, exit stroke lifts up towards next letter. Clues to slow writing: lots of separate strokes per letter, any serif that takes extra work, upright, no unevenness, every letter separate.

8 So you now have seven points of reference, but you are probably short of a few letters, and will have to make them up. Use your knowledge of the letters you do have – for example, make a missing 'q' by studying how 'a', 'o', and 'p' work. Think of any alphabet as a matching ensemble – all the letters have to look as if they belong to the same collection.

FELT-TIPPED PENS

Felt-tipped pens are convenient, inexpensive, and disposable
writing tools. Those which are designed for calligraphy come
with square-edged nibs, and in a selection of widths
and colours.

You will find felt-tipped pens are ideal for experimenting, for practising, and for producing fun items.

Use them for projects which will not be displayed in bright light, as the inks are often sensitive to light and may fade with time. With good quality pens, the nibs usually stay sharp for about the lifetime of the ink supply, if you do not press too hard. Some are supplied with two nib sizes, one at each end.

The convenience of felt-tipped pens and their bright colours make them worth considering for many quick projects which you do not intend to keep for a long time, such as the simple label shown here.

PROJECT

SIMPLE LABEL

You will need

- Felt-tipped square-edged pens, two colours, two sizes
- White paper or card
- Pencil, ruler, eraser
- Scissors or craft knife and cutting mat
- Plastic covering film (optional)

This design uses pens of two nib sizes, and two colours of ink. Try it this way first; then develop your own designs and consider variations in the colour scheme.

1 The best way to approach making a label with a decorative border is to write the name first. Attempting to fit a name into a ready-made border is much more difficult, and will result in poorly-formed lettering as you struggle to squeeze in, or spread out, the last few letters. Rule your guidelines and write the name carefully, positioning it well away from the edge of the paper or card so as to allow room for the border.

2 Once you have established the length of the name, measure equal distances all round the word and rule lines for the border. Try some experiments with the border patterns, keeping it simple but making several variants until you are satisfied with your design.

The examples shown here are all developed from the 'nib-width ladder' pattern, with added smaller squares, some set at right angles. Alternatively, use any of the patterns shown on pages 22–25, or develop your own.

When you have exhausted nib-width permutations, you could try repeated simple images.

3 When you have settled on your design, measure its depth and rule another line for the outer limit of the border pattern. Mark in the pattern all round, turning the paper as you tackle each side so that you are always holding the pen at the same angle – this will help you to achieve consistency in the squares. The corners may present you with difficulty in some designs – it is a good idea to practise a corner before you embark on the finished version!

4 Finally, trim out the page, leaving plenty of margin all round the border design. Labels such as this can be stuck inside books, hung on a child's bedroom door (if not in direct sunlight), or attached to containers or drawers. If they are likely to be splashed, for example in a kitchen, then cover the finished labels in self-adhesive plastic film as a protective measure.

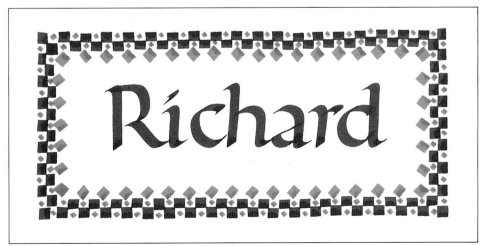

DIP PENS AND FOUNTAIN PENS

Many people start their calligraphic careers with a fountain pen, but dip pens are very popular and once you have discovered the versatility of dip pens, you will probably find that you want to use both.

FOUNTAIN PENS

The chief advantage of fountain pens is their convenience. The ink is often supplied in cartridges, which are easy to use and eliminates any spills on the carpet, and the pen will travel easily in a bag or pocket (but beware of leakage!).

They often are sold in a set with several sizes of nib, and some are provided with coloured ink cartridges in addition to the more common black variety. If you are planning to purchase one, look for a set which includes a nib of at least 2mm width.

Do not be confused if you see a nib described as an 'Italic'; you can use it for any style, it usually describes a fairly narrow nib which might be used for correspondence in neat Italic handwriting.

If you are left-handed, seek out left-oblique versions. They are often more easily obtainable in fountain pen sets than in dip pens.

A fountain pen works on the 'controlled leak' system, so that the ink is filtered through a lot of plastic before it reaches the end of the nib. This keeps the flow of ink smooth and constant, even when you are writing on a flat table.

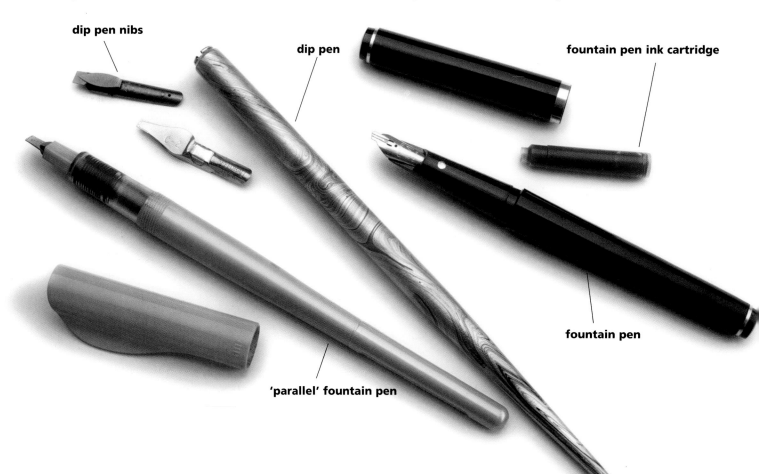

dip pen nibs

dip pen

fountain pen ink cartridge

fountain pen

'parallel' fountain pen

MAKING A TAPE RESERVOIR

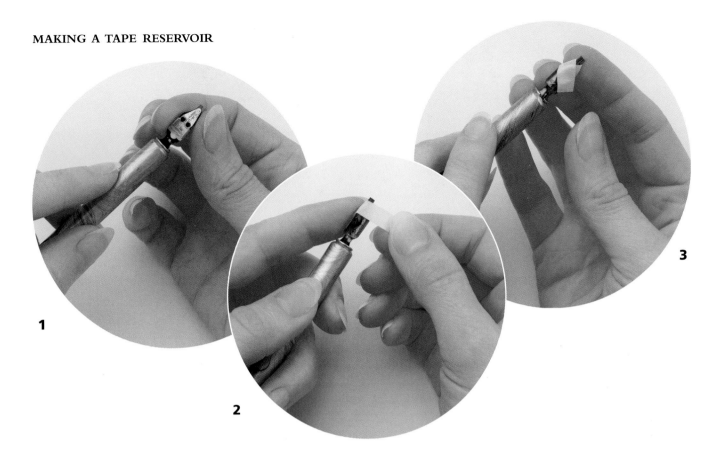

All that plastic becomes a disadvantage, however, when you want to change colour. Washing out a fountain pen sufficiently to prevent any residue from contaminating the next colour is the greatest challenge, so some manufacturers provide 'flushing-out' tools to help you with this task.

DIP PENS

There are many varieties made around the world, and you need to investigate what is available in your locality. Dip pens are easier to wash out than fountain pens, and they can be used with inks, watercolour paints and gouaches, so that very colourful projects can be undertaken. The nibs are generally made from thinner metal, resulting in sharper lettering. Most, however, need to be protected from rusting, unlike fountain pens.

Some dip nibs are made with left-oblique versions for left-handers.

There are also right-oblique nibs; these should be avoided by left-handers but they are popular with many right-handers, who find them helpful for Uncials, or any alphabet requiring a fairly flat pen angle. More advanced calligraphers find the right-oblique assists pen manipulation and twisting to achieve hairlines (very fine lines usually added at the end of a letter).

RESERVOIRS ON DIP PENS

1 A nib on its own can store very little ink or paint; although some do have a dimple in the top, which serves as a reservoir. Most pens have either fitted reservoirs on the top of the nib, or slide-on brass affairs that slip underneath. These latter cause considerable annoyance when they are too tight (they pinch the nib and prevent ink flow) or too loose (they fall off onto your work or disappear into your ink).

If you have similar trouble, you could try making a masking-tape reservoir:

2 Cut a thin strip of masking tape; check that the nib is dry or the tape will not adhere properly. Attach the tape as if bandaging a finger. Holding the tape in position with one finger, wrap the tape carefully around the nib. Remember that the wrapped area must ensure a good reservoir supply, with the leading edge touching the underside of the nib (so that the ink will be in contact with the slit in the nib).

3 Keeping the tape taut, continue to wrap the tape over itself to secure safely. With this fitted, you will have to feed the ink or paint into the reservoir with a brush, as dipping will make the tape soggy and it will eventually drop off. Always remove it when you have finished writing, as it will encourage rusting if left attached for long periods while wet.

Addressing Envelopes

Fountain pens or dip pens are suitable for these projects, though if you are using colour you may find that the dip pen is a little more productive. If your envelopes are thin enough to show lines through, you could prepare a lined card to slip inside as a guide. This will save you time if you devise a standard layout for envelope-writing.

Pictured left are three very different designs using two sizes of lettering with the name used as the prominent feature. Top: Name and address aligned left. Centre: Address set to the right to counterbalance the name. Below: Centrally placed.

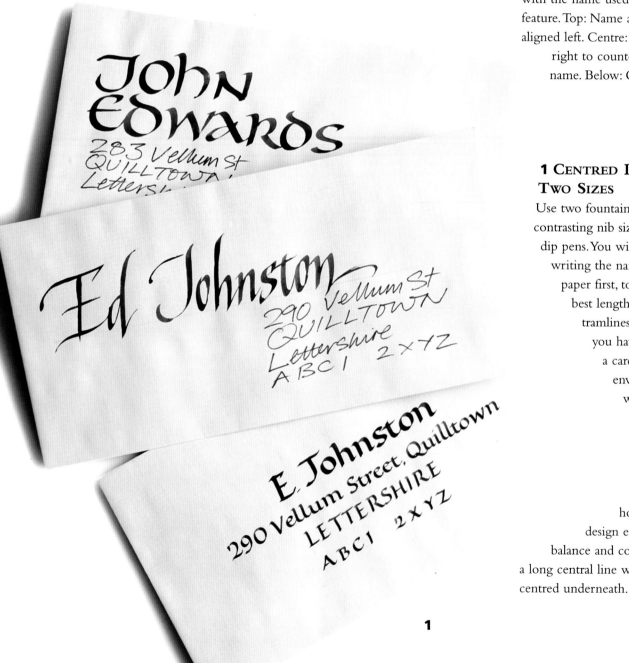

1 Centred Design in Two Sizes

Use two fountain pens set up with contrasting nib sizes, or use your dip pens. You will need to try out writing the name on rough paper first, to determine the best length. Then rule tramlines lightly, unless you have guidelines on a card inside the envelope. Practise writing the address in the smaller pen nib to check the length, and decide how it will fit. This design endeavours to balance and contrast by having a long central line with the postcode centred underneath.

1

2 ASYMMETRIC DESIGN IN TWO COLOURS

Now liven up and use the Uncial style with bright colours. Take advantage of their solidity to play with the colour inside. Write on a flat table rather than a sloping board so that the colour doesn't puddle to the bottom of the letters.

Write with a large pen in red, and while the ink is still wet, add drops of yellow to allow it to spread. You may have to stop after each letter to drop the second colour in. When completely dry, write in the address; you may wish to pencil it in first to ensure it will fit.

2

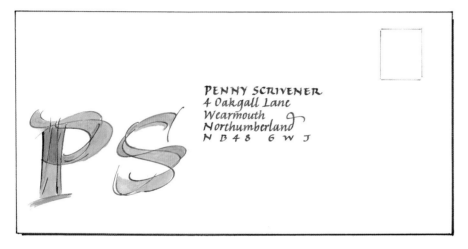

3

3 WILD CAPITALS

Not for the faint-hearted, these Versal-based capitals have to be written with a confident hand with lots of free movement. Use a thin dip pen with watered-down waterproof ink. Leave it to dry completely.

Write in the address neatly, using a narrow nibbed fountain pen perhaps, for ultimate contrast. Mix three very watery colours that look well together, and with a small paintbrush carefully fill in the shapes created by the free strokes.

4 COLOUR WITH GOLD PAINT

Try mixing cerulean blue with some gold gouache. Test it to see if there is sufficient gold to sparkle when it dries. Thoroughly load your pen so that plenty of colour is laid down (but take care about blots).

For a change, make the address the biggest part of the design, and write the name in a smaller pen.

4

USING BIG PENS

There are many occasions when the normal sizes of pens just described on the previous pages are too small to make an impact. For occasions when a large title or an eye-catching sign is needed, you will want bigger pens.

There are several kinds of pen to be found, although some are rather specialist and you may have to look in calligraphic society magazines for suppliers. But if you cannot find any, try writing with a piece of cardboard or balsa wood – this is how they look.

CARD LETTERS

Cut your card to fit the neck of your ink bottle, or decant the ink into a saucer. If you dip every time, you will get a blacker effect, but the grey half-tone look is quite effective. For a 'shadow' pen effect, cut a nick out of the edge of the card.

AUTOMATIC PEN

Similar to the Coit pen but with a rather more flexible nib, this comes in several sizes. The lettering shown here ranges from three nib-widths high upwards.

RULING PEN

This is a specialist ruling pen, but similar effects can be obtained by using a technical-drawing ruling pen held on its side to release more ink; it needs dipping after every stroke, and quick, confident, freestyle strokes. These are after the Italic style.

The thinner version is achieved by holding the pen higher up and using just its point.

specialist calligrapy ruling pen

technical drawing pen

COIT PEN

This pen has two 'bites' taken out of it to make those extra strokes (see example, below). It only comes in one size. Other Coit pens are solid-stroke pens available in various widths. This example shows heavyweight letters at less than the standard height.

coit pen

automatic pen

Making a Poster

You will need

- Large sheets of practice/layout paper
- Large sheets sturdier paper
- Automatic, Coit and ruling pens
- Colours – gouache or inks and paintbrushes
- Ruler, pencil, eraser

Try various weights to determine their impact. For a poster trying to attract the attention of passers-by, go for thick letters, here done at three and a half nib-widths high.

SALE

ALL THESE SHIRTS MUST GO TODAY

no reasonable offer refused

no reasonable

☥ SHIRTS

SALE

SALE

ALL THESE SHIRTS MUST GO TODAY

no reasonable offer refused

Sometimes a design will work either in 'portrait' or 'landscape' format, as shown here. If that is the case, then you should consult your client to decide which arrangement will best suit the site where it will be displayed. In any case, make your design catch the eye by crowding the text closely together, separated by size and style but not by white space – the job of white space is to encircle the writing to help the eye focus on the mass of text.

Using Big Pens **87**

If the poster is to be a one-off, you can afford to consider using colour. The colours used here were madder red (a red with a hint of magenta) and ultramarine blue. The top and bottom text are written in the pure red; the central text is ultramarine with a touch of the red, and with more red touched in with a paintbrush into each wet letter as soon as it was written.

If several posters are needed, the cheaper option would be to photocopy the artwork – which would mean black writing – perhaps onto a coloured paper.

THE CHISEL-EDGED BRUSH

The chisel-edged brush is ideal for large or chunky writing, and for use on surfaces which are not congenial to the pen (fabric, wood and plastic, for example). First you must get to know the tool – it is vital that you do not treat it like a pen.

The ancient Romans wrote their beautiful Capitals with a chisel-edged brush, working straight on to the stone for carving. The skills required to produce such letters, usually of several inches in height, are beyond the scope of this book. However, once you have developed some skill, the basic techniques of handling the brush are identical, whatever letterform you choose to write.

Most important: don't hold the brush like a pen! Hold it at the point on the metal ferrule where it changes from being flat to being round. Use your thumb and first two fingers, and twist the brush without your wrist moving. The edge of the brush must be positioned at right angles to the paper.

We rest our hand on the paper when we use a pen; you may instead need to rest your forearm for brush writing, as you must leave the hand free to keep the brush at right angles to the paper at all times. When you make a downstroke, your whole arm should move down.

Make your first experiments with gouache paint, mixed to a much thicker consistency than you would use for a pen. It should be like a thick cream (use an old brush for this). Wet the chisel-edged brush and squeeze it out, then load its edge with paint. Then, and this is vital, wipe the edge, on both sides, against the flat edge of the paint dish and inspect the fineness of the chisel end. You will probably need to load and wipe before each stroke.

1 Try a serif stroke: hold the brush at right angles to the paper, make the serif by a left-to-right movement followed by a smooth curve, pull downwards not forgetting to move your arm. When you feel confident with that, try some twisting. Note in the illustration how subtle changes in the thickness of the stroke are achieved by twisting the brush. Make the whole letter with a steady, even movement.

1

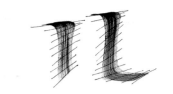

2

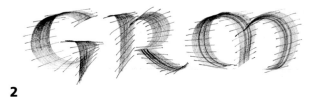

2 Uncial letters are ideal for brush treatment as they work well in 'chunky' form. Try them at three brush-widths high. Here are a few of the harder ones, where brush twisting makes the forms more subtle.

PROJECT

INSCRIBING A T-SHIRT

Practise writing with the brush, as shown above. Brown wrapping paper is cheap and effective to use for brush practice, as it has the kind of rough texture you might encounter on fabric. Study the Uncial hand (see page 36) and write it at three brush-widths. Then try even chunkier, at 2½ brush-widths. Remember to check your pen angle so you get thicks and thins where you want them.

You will need

- Brown wrapping paper
- T-shirt
- 6mm (¼ inch) and 13mm (½ inch) nylon lettering brushes
- Fabric paint
- Chalk
- Ruler
- Stiffening board
- Masking tape

'Smile' needs some emphasis and, as it is a small word, it can afford to be written with a wider brush. If you have chosen a mid-tone colour of T-shirt that will show up light as well as dark writing, try writing this in white.

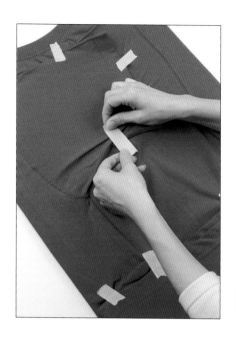

Now iron your T-shirt and put a stiffening board inside it. Check you have the front centrally positioned, then wrap the rest of the shirt round and tape it to itself.

Measure down from the shoulders of the T-shirt to get your guidelines straight. Mark your lines with chalk, or white pastel. Mark a central vertical line to help prevent the text drifting off course too much. Fold your final rough and tape it above where you plan to write.

Use fabric paint without thinning – decant a little into a dish, so you can keep flattening the brush edge as you charge the brush. Write the first line. You may have to go over it again to thicken up the paint. Don't be tempted to water down the paint as it may bleed into the fabric.

Write out all the text in the dark colour, before going back to do the white lettering. Wash out the brush well, as fabric paint may spoil it if left on the bristles while you write the other word. Select your larger brush, charge it with white and complete the word. When completely dry, rub off the chalk lines. Follow the instructions on the bottle to fix the paint – usually it requires you to iron on the reverse side of the fabric.

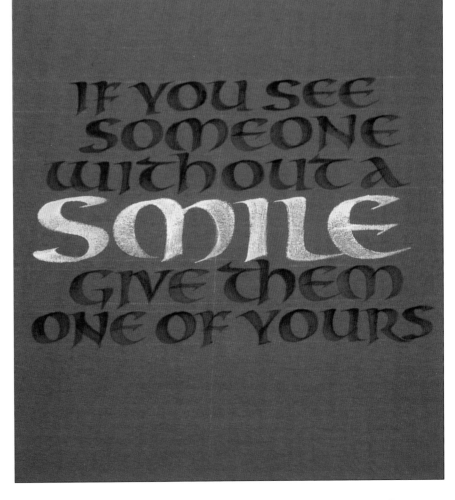

The final effect. Now think up your own slogan and try writing some more!

PRACTICE AND LAYOUT PAPER

For general practice and testing out rough designs, you need to have plenty of cheap but good quality paper.

Layout paper comes in pads – go for A3 size – which is about the size of this book when opened. It is very white and is thin enough to allow you to see writing, or ruled lines, on a sheet placed beneath.

The alternative is photocopying paper, but check it for compatibility with your ink first. A pad of layout paper containing 80 sheets costs about the same as an equivalent pad of cartridge paper containing 25 sheets, so you should feel happy to do lots of trials and practice runs without worrying about the cost.

If you find ruling lines a chore, then rule one page of lines very accurately, pressing harder than normal so they show up well, and slip it underneath as a template. This will not be as accurate as ruling on the page itself, but it can be useful as a starter. Remember to make sure that the lined sheet does not move!

BEWARE

BEWARE

Layout paper can save you time when preparing a design for which you need to practise and improve your letter spacing. Write out the chosen words, and assess them for spacing errors. Make marks where changes are needed. Place another sheet of layout paper on top, with guidelines ruled, trace over the words again, re-aligning the spacing as you go along. Here we see how the spacing before and after the letter W has been corrected.

The thin nature of layout paper makes it ideal for 'cut and paste'. Cut your lines of text and move them about on a fresh sheet of layout paper, gluing them down when you are satisfied with the design. To make certain, lest your eyes are deceived by the cut edges of the strips of paper, place another sheet of layout paper on top so you can see only the writing and not the individual strips of paper themselves.

When you are designing some lettering that could be flourished, it can be very helpful to write out the text first without any extensions. Then use overlay sheets of layout paper to draw some possible flourish designs with a pencil or pen. You can assemble several alternatives this way, without having to write the whole text out every time.

MAKING A CALLIGRAPHY NOTEBOOK

hhhhhhhaaannnnn
num ham man hum nan
ooocccddd bbbpppqq
deep pod bed code deep

You will need

- Your old practice sheets
- Scissors
- Notebook
- Craft glue and spreader
- Self-adhesive clear plastic (optional)

The only way to improve your calligraphy is to do a lot of writing! This will inevitably mean that you collect pages and pages of trial writing on layout paper. Before you decide to consign all this evidence of diligent work to the wastebin, take your scissors and cut out the best parts to keep.

Now find a notebook, or perhaps a ring binder, that you use for calligraphy notes. Lay it out flat to see how much area you need to cover, and spread out your selection of writing. Now put together some contrasting lettering – big capitals alongside small lower case for example, so that you can build up an interesting texture of design. Try placing them diagonally for more visual excitement.

Protect your tabletop, then spread glue generously over the reverse of the chosen pages. If the book has some images or writing on its cover, you will need to build up more than one layer of roughs to obscure any 'show-through'.

Fold the cover design over the edges of the notebook pressing it down on the inside of the cover and trim off any excess with scissors before the glue dries. Close the book while you glue the paper round the spine (if you glue it open, it will crack when closed).

For greater durability, when the glue is completely dry you can cover the whole with transparent self-adhesive plastic. This will prevent the writing from smudging, and will ensure that the edges of the papers do not lift.

CARTRIDGE PAPER

Once you have built up your confidence through writing on
practice papers, for a finished piece of work you will want to
use something which is a little thicker, but which is still cheap.
Cartridge paper fits this requirement.

It is one of the most common papers for drawing (often
sold in pads), and is used in art schools as an economical
paper that comes in large sheets.

Cartridge paper is made from wood pulp, and it may
turn slightly yellow with age. The surface is usually
suitable for calligraphy, if sufficient sizing to prevent the
ink from bleeding is applied, but there are many makes

available and it is best to experiment and ask the advice
of other users.

Go for the best quality you can afford, as some cheap
cartridge is slippery to write on. Choose 220gsm, which
is a sturdy thickness which will not show tiny 'bruises' if
handled carelessly.

Here is a project to try out using cartridge paper.

PROJECT

A GIFT BOOKLET

1

You will need

- Cartridge paper, 220gsm gauge
- Practice paper
- Pens, paints, paintbrush
- Pencil, ruler, eraser
- Potato and a small kitchen knife
- Glue
- Craft knife and cutting board

1 First practise your writing, once you have selected some
wording. This example is for a small gift that you might
send to a friend who needs your comfort. Practise the
words, then experiment with individual letters; having
selected Flourished Italic (see page 60) you will need to
explore to determine which possible variants to combine
in your chosen phrase.

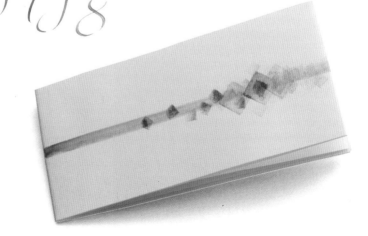

Reflect on your blessings

2

2 Here is an opportunity to take advantage of that long 'f', which reads the same either way up. The word 'reflect' also suggests the design solution. First write the phrase in green, making sure that the 'f' is very long and fluidly written. Turn over the page and change to blue. You may wish to write the 'e' first, in front of the 'f', then the R. Then complete the phrase as before.

3 Erase your pencil lines now. With a wide brush – or two strokes of a narrower one if necessary – draw a coloured stripe boldly along the 'x' height on each side. Make the mix more watery than it was for the writing. Cartridge paper, provided it is not too thin, will take a certain amount of paint successfully.

Reflect on your blessings

3

4 Now for some decorative fun: make some potato prints. Using a small kitchen paring knife, cut a small potato in half, then cut a few squares of different sizes in the surface for printing. Dip a square in the paint you were using, and do some test prints first to check its effect. You may want the paint to be a little thicker and stickier. If you have any, some gold gouache can add sparkle to some of the squares. The cartridge should take the prints well.

Reflect on your blessings

4

5 Trim the piece into a neat strip, and fold it down the centre. For the final presentation, you could cut another piece of cartridge for a cover, slightly larger all round than the piece of work. If the paper is a little flimsy, then cut a much longer strip, and fold back the ends to create a double-thickness cover.

Decorate the front in a similar way with a colour strip and potato prints (see opposite). Glue the inner to the cover along the folded crease. Put your name and an extra message on the inside back cover as a finishing touch.

5

WATERCOLOUR PAPERS

It is well worth investigating the benefits of watercolour
papers for calligraphy. They are made specifically to cope with
being made wet, which is not always the case with cheaper
cartridge paper. The gelatine sizing (or coating) which allows
it to accept this wetness also makes the letters applied in a
piece of calligraphy very sharp, so that the thick and thin
edges are clearly defined.

Such papers are ideal for making your own backgrounds, and these are shown on pages 126–127. All except very thick papers cockle if made very wet, so they should be stretched to prevent this (see pages 112–113), but this section deals with the use of watercolour papers in their plain state, for writing.

Some papers are whiter than others. Cautious artists favour the less white papers, as the bleaches used to whiten some papers may cause them to yellow with age. Bockingford and Saunders Waterford are reliable papers that are unlikely to cause any problems.

The best papers, such as some Fabriano papers, are made from 100 per cent cotton which makes it strong and durable. Wood pulp papers can also be of high quality depending on the source; and other papers are made from a combination of cotton and wood pulp.

The surface is usually gelatine sized, which makes it resist water or inks soaking in, and it also makes the surface resilient to the rubbing of a brush or eraser.

Watercolour papers come in a choice of thickness; this is measured in grams per square metre, gsm, or in pounds, lb. The most useful for calligraphers are 190gsm/90lb, and 300gsm/140lb. The project book shown overleaf was made with 190gsm paper.

Watercolour papers are manufactured for the specific needs of the watercolourist, and to this end there are three types of surface which are illustrated on these pages.

HOT PRESSED OR HP PAPER

This is very smooth, having gone through rollers to iron the surface flat (see below). For calligraphers, a very smooth surface is the most comfortable for writing, and owing to the excellent sizing, sharp writing

is almost guaranteed on these papers. There are some HP watercolour papers whose surface is very hard and unyielding, but this can sometimes be overcome by ensuring that there is a padded layer underneath when writing. Large writing can sometimes, as seen here, show up 'puddling', i.e. areas where the paint has settled into the bottom of the letters. This can be overcome by writing on a flat rather than sloped surface, and not raising the paper until it is dry.

NOT PAPERS

In other words, not hot pressed; this is the commonest form of watercolour paper, and is used by most watercolourists (see above). This is an exciting surface to use if you want a texture in the lettering; this is more likely to be wanted for large, rather than small, letters. Writing with a small pen is rather more difficult as the pen is fighting the bumpy surface. Washes are particularly controllable on this surface.

ROUGH PAPERS

Under some lights it is difficult to distinguish between Rough (below) and Not, but the surface is rougher than the Not, and is favoured by painters aiming for textural effects.

The pen can tell the difference; the surface is very resistant to writing. More pressure is needed just to allow any paint to flow from the pen. Writing with a small pen is particularly hard work and so will inhibit any letterform that relies on free-flowing script for its character.

MAKING AN ALPHABET BOOK

You will need

- Watercolour paper
- Heavier, perhaps hand-made, paper for cover material
- Automatic pen
- Gouaches
- Mixing paintbrush and finer paintbrush
- Ruler, pencil, eraser
- Craft knife and cutting mat
- Hole punch and gold paper fastener

This is a fun kind of book, of no particular practical use, which just rejoices in the texture of the paper and the roundness of the uncial letters, while also playing with colours.

1 Rule lines and write out the alphabet in a large pen to decide how many letters will fit per line. These letters are written at two and a half nib-widths height, for extra chunkiness, but you can try other weights. Work out all the measurements before getting to work on the watercolour paper.

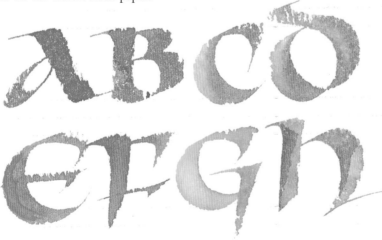

2

2 Using scarlet and lemon yellow, write boldly first with the red paint in a large pen. Feed some yellow into the pen after the first few letters, and carry on mainly in red with occasional yellow 'contamination'.

3 When all the letters have been written, mix some watery paints to fill in some of the shapes between; bring in some magenta, but remember to keep it watery. Use it to fill a few shapes.

Mix watery magenta with the lemon yellow for a nearly pink flesh colour. There is no need to fill every gap – leave some white areas too.

Complete the design by making a wash at the right-hand edge; paint clear water up to the edge of the paper, then introduce one of the colours along the edge nearest the letter and be careful to graduate it as you move outwards.

3

4

4 Cut the strips with a sharp craft knife on a board. Cut two similarly sized strips of another thick paper – handmade paper has been used here – to make the covers. Use an office hole-punch to put a hole in the end of each strip – mark on the punch where the edge of the paper should be aligned, so that all the leaves have their holes in the same position. Fasten the whole book together with a paper fastener.

COLOURED PAPERS

Coloured papers are a delight to use, and many inexpensive
sorts are available. Some examples are shown overleaf.

If they have a smooth surface, they will probably accept calligraphy, but if you are unsure, buy just a single sheet to test its quality first. Some coloured papers intended for use with pastels have a surface texture, and these can be fun to use for calligraphy too. Others, Ingres papers especially, have faint lines across them. They are also intended for pastels, and they come in subtle greys and browns.

Most of these papers are cartridge-type products, which are made from dyed pulp, or which are dyed after manufacture. Not all dyes are light-fast, so it is possible that your paper may eventually fade if displayed in strong light. But this does not usually deter calligraphers, who enjoy experimenting and are prepared to take the risk.

THICKNESS
Many of these papers are quite thin, which means you must take care when handling them as their vulnerability to 'bruising' is greater than watercolour papers, for instance, which are thicker. Hold the sheet up to the light – support it with two hands or you will bruise it even more – and look for the tell-tale signs: little creases which cannot be removed (except by stretching – see page 112). Always keep your papers flat, preferably between stiff boards. Some papers can be bought in pads of mixed colours, and this is a safe way to keep them in good condition.

PROJECT

A PERPETUAL CALENDAR

Here is a project using several colours of papers – to show off their variety – for the creation of a perpetual calendar. It is ideal for permanently recording birthdays and anniversaries.

You will need

- Pens and ink
- Pad of mixed-colour pastel papers, 229mm x 153mm (9in x 6in)
- Backing paper, 153mm x 420mm (6in x 16 ¹/₂in)
- Pencil, ruler, eraser
- Fine liner fibre-tip pen or ruling pen
- Craft knife and cutting mat
- Glue, hole punch, thread

1 Measure and cut all the pages to the same size, as shown in the diagram, and rule lines for the month and the days. If you buy a pad of mixed Ingres colours measuring 229mm x 153mm (9 x 6in), they need only be cut in half to fit these measurements (and the top trimmed off if the pad is spiral bound).

The great advantage of this kind of calendar is you do not have to work out how the numbers change relative to the days of the week, so each month's block will be the same except that you leave out certain dates for those months that have fewer than 31 days.

2 Write the name of the month along the bottom of the sheet, in black ink, in the centre. There is a considerable difference in width between the names of the months – May and December for instance – so either choose to write in a freely flourished Italic (when you are experienced enough), or select a more formal style and fill up the spaces either side with pen patterns.

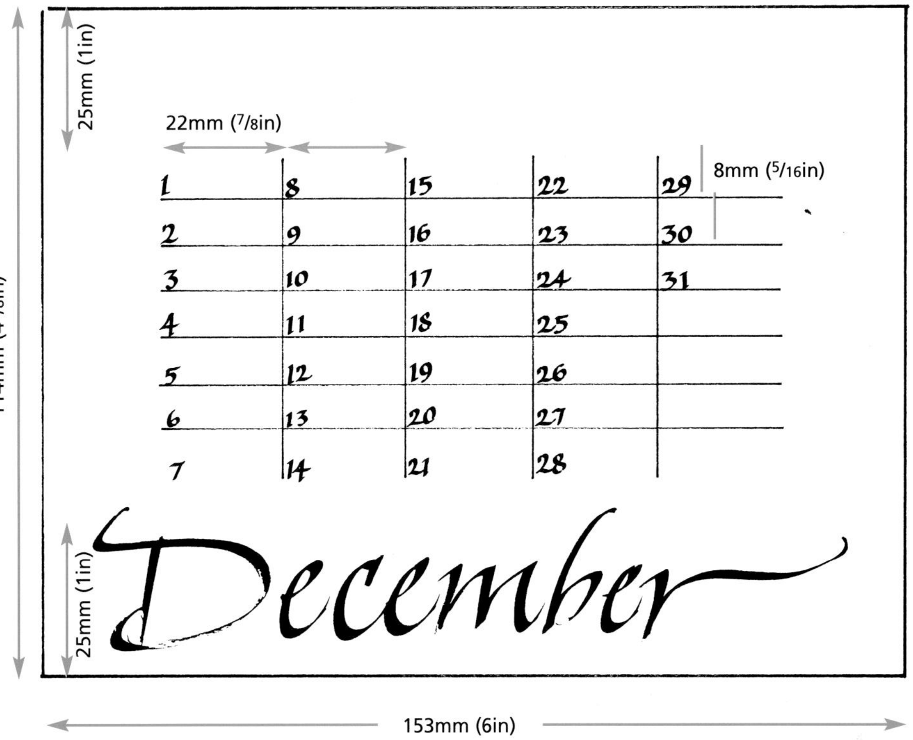

With a smaller pen, write in the numbers in the corners of the date boxes remembering to leave enough space for the user to add the names of friends and relatives. Rule the lines with a fine liner fibre-tip pen or a technical ruling pen. Do this for all the months. Finally, put a crease along the upper edge, 25mm (1in) from the top of the page.

3 & 4 Complete a trial page to check that all the measurements are working. Rule the lines in pencil before committing to the pen, and mark how many days there are for each month, so you don't do too many! If you are unhappy with any writing, you have only lost one page not the whole calendar.

3

4

When you have completed all the months, decide how you want the cover to appear. In this example, there is one large word for the title with some smaller writing below.

Do some trials on practice paper before committing yourself to the coloured paper. If anything goes wrong, scribble the corrections over the top and copy from that for the final version.

5 Now you need to glue the calendar sheets together onto some backing paper. Cut a sheet of paper to the measurements shown below, and mark all the way down where each monthly page is to be attached.

Start gluing from the bottom, beginning with December. Finish with the cover, and punch some holes in the top through which you can thread a hanging tape.

THE FINISHED CALENDAR
The final effect works well using a selection of subtle colours such as can be found in a pad of Ingres pastel papers. Of course, you can use brighter colours if you want the calendar to catch your eye when on display.

5

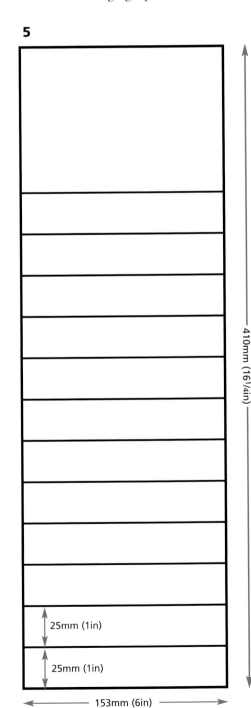

25mm (1in)

25mm (1in)

410mm (16¼in)

153mm (6in)

HAND-MADE PAPERS

Hand-made papers can be obtained from art supply shops, and they are available in many colours and textures. It is not possible to write on them all, because many have a rough surface or have too 'busy' a pattern or texture.

Others have leaves or coarse fibres embedded in them which can catch the nib of the pen, or insufficient sizing is used in their manufacture, resulting in the ink bleeding into the paper. Yet, despite all these difficulties, such papers are loved and used by calligraphers.

When they defeat the pen, they serve beautifully as book endpapers or covers (as on page 99), and when they are smooth enough to take the pen, and plain enough to avoid visual distraction, they are valued for their wonderful subtlety.

Hand-made papers can usually be recognized as such by their rough edges, called the deckle edge. This indicates that they were made as single sheets rather than on a continuous roll. Paper made by machine in a continuous roll will be reliably consistent in thickness and surface texture, and thus ideal for many projects. The attraction to artists and calligraphers of hand-made papers lies in the individuality of every sheet. While you may confuse some plain white or cream hand-made papers with the machine-made versions, you are less likely to be confused by the decorative papers, especially those with plant material embedded in the surface. If you need several sheets for a project, you should first check their colour match as every sheet and every batch will vary.

Hand-made papers are produced all over the world, and each example has its own character. Some of the most unusual are made with plant-based fibres, such as bark, leaves, bamboo, straw, or bracken.

They naturally cost a little more than a similarly sized sheet of machine-made paper, because they are individually made and cater for a more specialist market.

WRITING ON HAND-MADE PAPER

First test a small area of the paper to see if the ink bleeds. Write in the ink or paint you intend to use, and notice also how the surface feels to the pen – is it slippery? It may be highly polished, and you may have to press harder to produce good letters. Does the pen catch on fibres? If thin, loose fibres are present on the

surface, the pen will lift them and the ink will bleed into that area, so take extra care with your pen pressure. Is the surface lumpy? Bigger pens will skim over the pits and produce an attractive textured letter, but small nibs may catch on every pit.

Or try writing with a brush instead! Does the surface seem rather soft? This may make erasing your lines difficult or even impossible, as you will remove some of the soft surface at the same time. So rule your lines very lightly and avoid any overlap into areas where you will not write.

1 Some hand-made papers look like pictures already. The Indian straw paper pictured on the previous page brings windy weather to mind, and here some suitable text has been written on a plainer area. It is curved to blend with the shapes already present in the paper. However, the writing is rather overwhelmed by the paper's texture, and it is illustrated here to alert you to the potential problems of choosing 'busy' paper on which to write. In order to stand up to the background, the text here needs to be stronger in colour, weight or size, and possibly all three.

PROJECT

MAKING A COLLAGE

When you have developed a collection of hand-made papers, you may find it hard to decide what to do with them! One day, however, the right quotation will turn up to get you started.

Hand-made papers are very individual, and so you probably only have one sheet of the more unusual examples, and you will not want to waste it. This is where a collage will prove economical.

Do all your planning and practising on layout paper, and work out a design which uses small strips of writing, so you don't use too much of your paper, especially if you make mistakes.

1 Begin by writing out the text a few times to become acquainted with the words, and to decide on any emphasis. This is part of a Shakespeare sonnet, and its wintry text lends itself to some of these papers, as several of them have dried leaves or other plant material in them. Once you have decided on a letterform – Italic Capitals are the choice here (see pages 52-53) – experiment with combinations of sizes for emphasis.

You will need

- Hand-made papers
- Dip pens and gouache
- Craft knife and cutting mat
- Layout paper
- Pencil, ruler, eraser
- Glue

Write out the whole piece on layout paper and make a paste-up (see page 154 if you have not yet tackled paste-up) to settle on your design before using too much of your special paper.

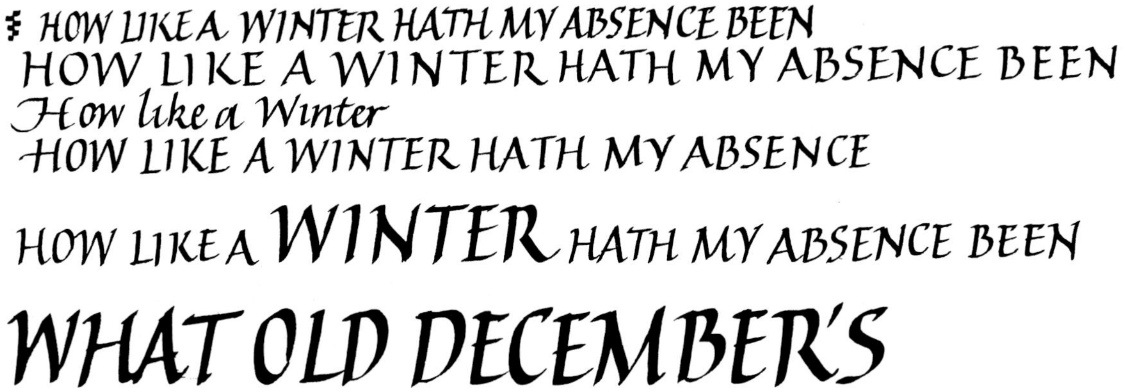

HOW LIKE A WINTER HATH MY ABSENCE BEEN
HOW LIKE A WINTER HATH MY ABSENCE BEEN
How like a Winter
HOW LIKE A WINTER HATH MY ABSENCE

HOW LIKE A WINTER HATH MY ABSENCE BEEN

1 *WHAT OLD DECEMBER'S*

2 When you are well ahead with your design, try out some of the papers that you might use; don't choose anything too rough for your first project – save that for the background!

These examples use Khadi straw paper (not the same as the busy straw example shown on the previous page), and another Khadi paper made with banana leaves. Brown ink blends well with the paper and suits the text (for those living in the northern hemisphere, at least!)

If you find that the surface is a little soft and tends to make the paint bleed, try spraying the surface with fixative or hairspray (a cheaper alternative) before you start to write.

3 Write out the text on strips of hand-made paper; if you make a mistake, you only have one phrase to redo, not the whole piece. Then lay them onto various papers to see what looks best.

At this stage, make some margin guides out of strips of paper held at 90°, so you can see just how the text will fit and how the margins affect the design. When you are satisfied with your design, glue the strips down securely.

2

3

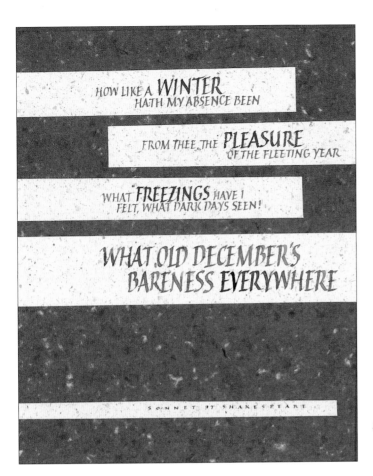

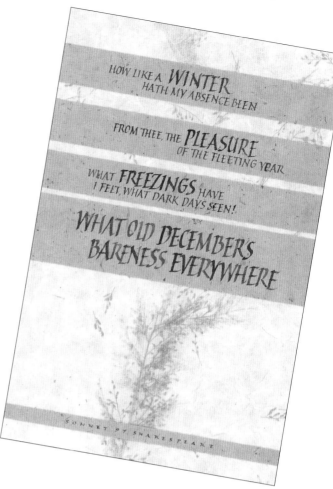

4 For a dramatic version, this black paper has white specks and it throws the banana-paper strips into sharp relief. For added drama, the strips of text are trimmed to break up their shapes. The positioning relative to the margins is important, so again if you are trying this version, keep some dark strips available to decide the margins as you lay it out.

5 An alternative design, using an unusual paper which has grass seed-heads embedded in the surface as the background. This would have been too bumpy to write on, but it serves to add a pictorial element to the design – the choice of paper for the text is a darker colour than the straw or banana paper, selected in order to provide some contrast to the background.

TEARING, FOLDING AND CUTTING

Many of the projects described in this book require you to
cut or trim paper, or to fold and sometimes tear it. It is
worthwhile getting to know the best ways to do this,
so as to avoid the common pitfalls.

A sharp fold, a rough edge used to effect, and crisply
trimmed work will enhance your presentation
tremendously.

GRAIN DIRECTION

'Grain' in this sense refers to the direction of the fibres in
the paper. Hand-made, or mould-made papers do not have
a grain direction, as the fibres are laid randomly. In machine-
made papers, however, the fibres become aligned in one
direction along the length of the machine, rather like the
warp threads in machine-woven fabric. Paper is stronger
along the grain direction. This affects tearing and folding.
To find out which way it is made, try these methods.

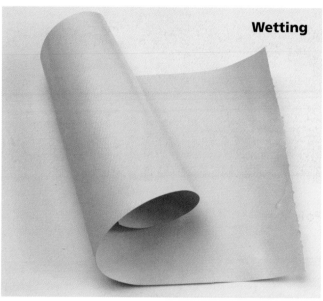

Wetting

Grain direction

Gently curve machine-made paper and push along it with
your hands, first one way then the other; you will feel
more resistance one way; the stronger grain resists folding
(see photograph above).

If you can spare a piece to ruin in the cause of science,
wet it and see which way it curls. The grain lies along the
straighter, not the curling, direction.

TEARING

To tear machine-made paper, try first with something you
are willing to sacrifice, and tear it both ways. You will find
it easier to tear along the grain, but the tear pattern will
be more interesting against the grain. Notice if the paper
tends to tear in layers, giving you a width of raw edge.

Tearing hand-made papers is more unpredictable; some
are very strong and resistant to tearing. Another method is
to wet the paper first, by running a paintbrush of clean
water against a ruler down the line you wish to tear; then,
when the water has soaked in, you can pull the sides apart
(see photographs on opposite page).

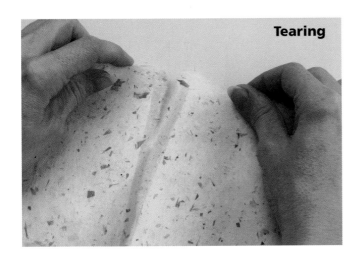

Tearing

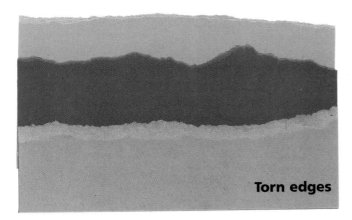

Torn edges

Folding

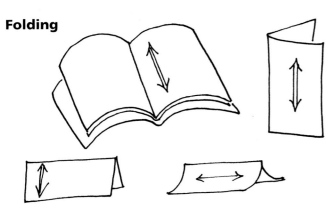

FOLDING

Most thin papers will fold without much trouble, and without any tool. However, when you use substantial paper or card, you need to use a folding tool, and it is important to know the paper's grain direction.

Before folding, consider the purpose of the item. If you are folding pages for a book, the grain must allow the pages to flop open, so the grain must be aligned with the fold. If it is a card, intended to stand up with the fold vertical, keep the grain aligned as in the book. But if the card is to bear a fold along the top, you need the paper to be stiff in the direction from table to crease, otherwise it

will flop over on display (see diagrams below left). When you have established your grain direction, and ruled lines for folding, use a pointed but blunt instrument, such as a knitting needle, or better still a bookbinder's 'bone folder', to run along the line against a ruler, on the inside of the card or book page.

CUTTING

Invest in a craft knife and plenty of spare blades. Here's the health warning – blunt blades make you press harder, pressing hard makes you slip, a slipped knife on fingers hurts, and gets a lot of blood on your paper... Use a ruler with a metal edge or a metal ruler. If you cut against the normal ruler you use for drawing your lines, you'll soon need to buy a new one as you will inevitably damage the edge. Keep a backing board from a layout pad as your cutting surface, or invest in a 'self-healing' cutting mat the surface of which reforms after the blade has passed through it. Always position the ruler so that you can cut by pulling the knife towards your body, ensuring that your supporting hand is never in the way, as it would be if the the ruler were horizontal.

If the paper is thick, press hard on the ruler, but use repeat strokes with the blade rather than try to do it in one go (and remember the warning given above about pressing hard).

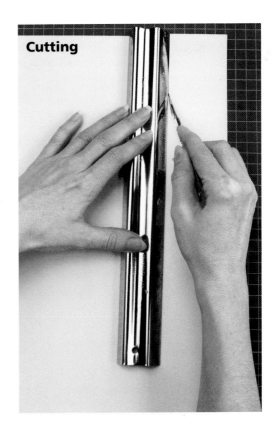

Cutting

MAKING GREETINGS CARDS

Just one or two words is all you need to make an eye-catching card, using coloured papers or tissue arranged in layers for decoration. Start by assembling your papers, so you can decide on the colour, or colours, to use for the text.

1 Practise your wording a few times, then write the message on good paper. For the multi-coloured effect, touch the second colour in with a fine paintbrush while each letter is still wet.

Use a craft knife on a mat to trim the strip of writing, when you are sure it is dry. Then lay this over some coloured tissue and tear it to shape – if it is tough to tear, use a paintbrush with clean water to wet a line all round where it needs to be torn, then try again. Mount these elements onto an orange background and trim and fold into a card.

You will need

- Coloured papers or tissue which blend well together
- Thicker paper or card
- Dip pen and gouache/watercolour paint
- Pencil, ruler, eraser
- Creasing tool (knitting needle)
- Craft knife
- Cutting mat
- Craft glue
- Novelty scissors (optional)

1

2

2 Alternatively, when you have written the word, trim the card with novelty scissors and run a paintbrush charged with gold paint along the edges. Do the same with a larger piece of orange paper, and mount both onto white. Trim and fold into a card.

3 Try some picture-making with torn papers and pastels. Cut an orange semi-circle, rub orange and grey pastels across the paper to create an evening sky effect, and paste the orange shape in place like a setting sun.

4 Tear some thin papers into interesting shapes to make overlays suggesting hills; when you are satisfied with the effect, glue them down. Practise your Versals and write your message ('Time Flies'). Fold and trim the card to size

3

4

TIME
FLIES

STRETCHING PAPER

If you intend to make your paper wet, perhaps by making a
colour wash background, but don't want a wrinkled end
product, then you will need to stretch the paper first.

This takes a little time, but is well worth the effort – ironing wrinkly paper just
isn't the same!

1 Wet the paper thoroughly by running it under a tap or soaking it in the bath.
Lay it carefully onto a plywood board. When paper is soaked, it relaxes and
becomes slightly larger – and wrinkly. Stretching involves taping it down while
it is larger, so that it dries flat. Wet the brown tape and stick the paper down
firmly, taping opposite sides first, and pulling the paper out as flat as you can.

You will need

- Piece of plywood, larger than your sheet of paper
- Watercolour paper
- Brown 'Butterfly' parcel tape
- Craft knife
- Wash brush and paint

2 Leave the board to dry naturally. Lay it flat, rather than
propping it up, to prevent over-wetting one strip of tape.
As it dries, the paper should shrink back to its original
size and thus be tensioned against the tape. When it is
successfully stretched, it should not wrinkle as much when
you apply your wash. Sometimes, if the tape is not well
secured, it will pull away from the paper as it dries, as
shown and you will have to repeat the process.

WHITE ON DARK WASH

PROJECT

3 Lay your wash. Mix up sufficient colour to complete
the job, and fill your wash brush to capacity. Tilt the board
slightly and start at the top in confident strokes, with
plenty of paint or water in the brush at all times.

4 To achieve a 'stormy sky' kind of background, start with
strong colour at the top and replenish the brush with
water as you work down the page. Add another layer and
leave the board flat to dry.

5 When the wash is completely dry, you can cut it off the
board inside the taped edges. Do not remove it until you
are sure you have finished applying washes, and it has dried.
Use a steel rule and a sharp knife, and cut towards you.

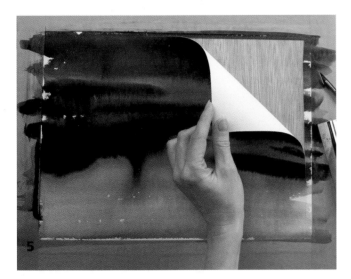

The best way to remove the brown tape from the board is to wet it and scrape it off.

6 Select the best area of wash to work on and write your wintry text. If the background is very busy, you may find it difficult to achieve enough contrast so that the writing will show up. For this Shakespearean extract, use bleedproof white against the dark blue skyscape.

7 The completed piece.

COLOURED INKS

Coloured inks are generally supplied in bottles at a consistency that is ready to use. Their colours are vibrant and attractive, and fun to use. Like watercolours, they are normally transparent, and so they look best on white paper.

Take care to read the labels before buying, to check if they are waterproof or not. Most of these inks are dye-based, making them staining in nature, but the colours may fade if left permanently on display.

WATERPROOF COLOURED INKS
Check the labels; if acrylic or shellac is mentioned, then this is waterproof. Waterproof inks must not be allowed to dry on your pen or it will clog and you will have difficulty in cleaning

it. Waterproof inks are often thicker than non-waterproof ones, which makes writing with clean sharp edges difficult unless you thin it.

The very best use for waterproof inks is for wash backgrounds (see pages 126–129), because when the surface dries it forms a seal and helps prevent the writing on top from soaking into the surface and so causing 'bleeding'. Use the inks watered down as if they were watercolours.

NON-WATERPROOF COLOURS
These are ideal for the dip pen, and some are formulated especially for fountain pens. For the latter you can buy cartridges, but these tend to employ more watery inks (which are thus less bright) than the bottled versions. Be warned – if you have used black ink in a fountain pen, you will have problems in washing it out sufficiently well to allow a change to a coloured cartridge. Muddy colours will result.

PROJECT

A FUN BOOKMARK

You will need

- Three colours of ink, non-waterproof
- Dip pens
- Wide paintbrush
- Ruler, pencil, eraser
- Coloured paper/card for mount
- Self-adhesive plastic

1 Try out this idea using just three non-waterproof colours (you want them to run) – turquoise, green and orange are shown here, but you can choose any you like.

1

2 With the same pen still loaded with the blue ink, rule a rough line along a ruler and immediately wash a wide, wet paintbrush across it to smudge the line. With smaller pens, using the other colours, make quick strokes upward from the wet area while the strip is still wet – it looks rather as if reeds are growing out of a pond!

2

3

3 Now you are ready to assemble everything. Write the message first. When it is dry, erase the pencil guidelines and make the blue stripes along the bottom. Try adding green too for more depth of design, but keep it wet. With the smaller pens add the reeds/flowers which make the letters start to look as if they are lost in the wilds. Note how transparent these inks are, a quality which adds to their attraction.

4 Finally, cut a mount in bright blue paper or cut out the artwork and glue it onto a wider strip of blue. This will stiffen it and finish it off. You could cover it with clear self-adhesive plastic if you want it to be durable. **4**

BLACK INKS

Black inks come in various forms, but not all of them produce
good results in a calligraphy pen. Most calligraphers carry out
all their trials and practice in black, and you will soon find
that you develop a favourite which works well for you on
your usual paper with your usual pen.

NON-WATERPROOF INK

This is the best form to use for most
occasions, provided the work will not
be exposed to splashing or rain.
Non-waterproof inks generally have
a good consistency for the dip pen.

Fountain-pen inks are dye-based
and can be rather watery but they are
useful for practising with a dip pen
because they flow so easily. They can
be found in stationery stores.

However, for a good dense black,
visit your art supplies shop and look
for black inks made in China or
Japan, usually sold in large black
plastic bottles. (Or try a supplier of
Chinese goods.) You can dilute these
with water as some come in
concentrated form.

Black gouache is an excellent and
economical form of ink; use it when

you are doubtful of the paper surface,
as it is the least likely form of ink to
bleed.

Alternatively, experiment with the
various inks available for calligraphy,
but read the label carefully and check
for shellac or acrylic in the
ingredients as this indicates that the
ink will dry waterproof.

'PERMANENT' INKS

Some black inks are labelled as
permanent, and this gives rise to
confusion. Does it mean it will not
fade in bright light, or it will not
come out of your clothes because it's
dye-based, or it will not smudge
when dry?

Permanence in paints refers to its
lightfastness, and you should assume
this is the case with black inks – but

it may also indicate that it stains and
is waterproof, so check the label
further!

WATERPROOF INKS

These are usually either acrylic based,
or contain shellac. Some are rather
thick to use in a dip pen, which will
make crisp writing difficult; thinning
with water is possible but don't
overdo it or the finished result will
look grey because it has lost its
density. Generally these inks are not
recommended except when the need
for the work to be smudge-proof is
greater than the need for sharp
writing. Take care to prevent the ink
from drying on the nib, as it will be
difficult to remove and will clog the
pen. Never use this ink in a fountain
pen.

PROJECT

A PRESENTATION BOOKPLATE

You will need

- Black ink • White paper
- Ruler, pencil, eraser
- Layout paper
- Craft knife and cutting mat
- Scissors and paste

Black ink on crisp white paper is
ideal for formal occasions such as
when making a presentation to
someone to commemorate long
service. Try your version of the label
shown opposite for insertion in a
favourite book.

1 ✒ 𝕲𝖊𝖔𝖗𝖌𝖊 𝕭𝖆𝖒𝖇𝖚𝖗𝖞

✒ on the occasion of

✒ on the occasion of his retirement

2 To make a centred design, cut out the strips of text, and paste them in position across a central vertical line; this is your master copy (see pages 92-93 for more on 'paste-up'). At this stage, it looks as if the contrast between the two sizes of pen used is not enough; write the name again in a larger size on another strip and paste it over. When you are satisfied with your design, select your paper, bearing in mind the thickness of the pages in the book. If the paper you choose has an identifiable grain direction (see pages 108-9), make sure it will curve with the page of the book. Rule all the lines lightly on the final paper, and mark where the text starts and ends on each line.

3 Now write the text carefully, line by line, checking with your master copy frequently. If the paper you are using is thin enough, which it may need to be if it is to be pasted into a book, you may be able to lay it over your master and more or less trace it – this will prevent your writing from stretching wider than the original version, which sometimes happens.

Paste it into the book using a glue which doesn't wet the paper too much (or it will wrinkle).

1 First, perform some size trials and decide which script will be best. Foundational is formal, and would usually meet the need, but for this Bible Studies Society the Gothic hand seems appropriate. Write out all the text so that you can work out how it will fit.

2

Presented to
𝕲𝖊𝖔𝖗𝖌𝖊 𝕭𝖆𝖒𝖇𝖚𝖗𝖞
on the occasion
of his retirement as
secretary of the
Bible Studies Society
of Portsmouth

J U N E 2 0 0 1

3

WATERCOLOUR PAINTS

Watercolour paints have many uses in calligraphy, both for
producing backgrounds and for writing. Good quality paints
are very lightfast, and provide vibrant colours.

It is important to remember that watercolour paints are transparent – designed specifically for watercolour artists to get subtle colour build-up by overlaying thin colours. For calligraphers that means that they work best on white paper; if you write in watercolour on a coloured stock, the background colour will show through.

SPRINGTIME

Transparency is a key feature of watercolours, as shown here. To try this for yourself, use a brush to lay down streaks of blue and leave them to dry. Write on top in green, letting the letters cross from the white to the blue – you will see the blue background through the green letters.

If you want stronger lettering against the background, then gouaches are needed for their opacity (see pages 130–3).

PROJECT

A DECORATED NAME

You will need

- Large pen
- Watercolours
- Watercolour paper or good cartridge paper
- Small paintbrush
- Ruler, pencil, eraser

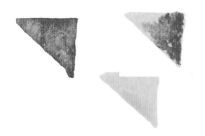

Try this fun way to present someone's name – anybody would be delighted to receive such a gift. First write the name with a large pen, in ultramarine, and leave it to dry.

The opposite colour to blue is orange, and here you can use orange to make a very bright design – but to vary its texture, and to avoid a jarring effect, mix the orange unevenly. Prepare carmine and Winsor yellow paints, both to the same consistency.

Paint some of the areas with carmine, and while still wet, drop some of the yellow in with another paintbrush, so that it mixes unevenly on the page.

In other areas, lay the yellow first, and carmine afterwards. The end result will be variable oranges with yellows and reds – much more fun than flat orange!

gouache

watercolour

pan

watercolour

gouache

Tubes of watercolour paint are smaller than tubes of gouache. Watercolour pans are sold individually and can easily be added to your paint box.

TUBES OR PANS?

Watercolour paints are sold in two forms: in small cakes
known as 'pans' or 'half pans', and in tubes. Both types are
equally good – but don't be deceived into buying poster
colours (which also come in cakes) by mistake.
Poster paints are cheap children's colours which are
too coarse for calligraphy.

If you plan to do washes for
backgrounds, tubes may be best, as
you will need a good quantity of
paint at a time; the pans are better for
small amounts because you wet them
and rub off only as much you need
with your brush. You will also require
a palette for mixing, and several sizes
of paintbrush.

LIGHTFASTNESS

Watercolour paint manufacturers
generally have a coding system on the
labels, showing how well the pigment
stands up to exposure to light.
Depending on the manufacturer, it
may say 'Lightfastness 1' or 'Permanence
A' if the pigment is resistant to fading.

Most watercolours are fade-
resistant, with the exception of some
reds. This is even true of printing
inks which are meant to resist fading
– note how the red disappears on
coloured posters which have been on
display outdoors for several months. If
the label says Permanence C, use the
paint only for projects which are not
intended for long-term display.

1 The strip on the left was exposed
to light in a sunny window for nine
months and the control strip on the
right was stored in the dark. Note

how some of these colours have
faded from the half which was
exposed to bright light.

TRANSPARENCY/OPACITY

Watercolour paints are generally
transparent. Some pigments are a
little opaque, but all are intended to
be used thinly, with plenty of water.

This means that you can see
through them. If the colour
underneath is white, you just see the
pure colour, but if the underlying
background is a colour, then it will

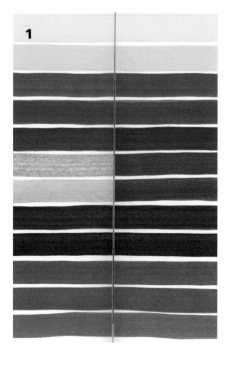

affect the colour on top – yellow
will turn greenish over a blue, for
example.

Where opacity is needed, then
choose gouache paints (see pages
130-133). The colours of watercolour
paints are strong, and so you need
only minute quantities, which is why
the tubes are small. You mix them
with quite a lot of water. They are
excellent for making background
washes, as they leave no sediment,
unlike gouaches which have a lot
of 'body'. A gouache background has
an absorbent surface, which is
difficult to write on. Writing on top
of a watercolour wash is best done in
gouache paints, unless a see-through
effect is desired.

If you are writing on good quality
white paper, however, watercolours
give excellent results, as their
transparency over the white shows
off the colours in their full vibrancy.

2 Watercolour graded wash with
gouache lettering.

STAINING AND GRANULATING

As watercolours are used thinly,
especially in washes, their other
properties, particularly how they stay
on the page, are noticeable. Some

colours (often reds) will stain the paper, so that if you decide to try to remove some colour by washing it out, you may be unsuccessful.

Some colours, when mixed with others, make granular or mottled effects – cobalt, rose madder, and sometimes ultramarine do this. It is most noticeable on a textured paper where the colours separate out and settle into the grain of the paper.

2

3 Ultramarine wash showing granulating effect.

LIFTING OFF MISTAKES

If you write some text and find you have made an error, there is usually nothing for it but to start again. But sometimes, if it's quite a small error such as one letter needing to be replaced by another of the same width, and the text is written in watercolour on good quality paper, you could try washing it out.

First, protect the rest of the design by covering it with a sheet of thin paper, from which you have cut a small hole to expose the part to be corrected. Use a scrupulously clean brush with equally clean water and a piece of clean kitchen towel.

With the damp brush, gently wet the offending letter and dab it immediately with the kitchen towel. Keep repeating this process, so that you thin down the colour. If it's not a staining colour, you should be able

3

to wash it out. Take care not to roughen the paper surface by rubbing at it.

Leave it now to dry completely – or use a hair dryer if time is short. If you write on top while it is the slightest bit damp, the letter will spread as if written on blotting paper.

Before attempting to write the correction, use a smooth object like a teaspoon to burnish the surface and press down the paper fibres; this will help to repair the surface and should prevent bleeding when you write. In example **4**, the replacement 's' has blobbed a little at the bottom, where the paper was more roughed-up by the washing process.

Mix your paint for writing in the correction, adding a little gum Arabic to the paint to help stop it spreading if the paper surface has become absorbent. Do a trial letter on another sheet to check for colour consistency, and then write in the correction.

4

ALL YOU NEED TO KNOW ABOUT COLOUR

Colour can do wonders for your calligraphy,
especially if you know what you're doing! Have fun
writing in all the colours of the rainbow.

RAINBOW
Draw a circle with a compass, and rule lines radiating from the centre 40° apart (i.e. 360° divided by nine).

Prepare all the colours shown on the triangle opposite, and write a word in each colour.

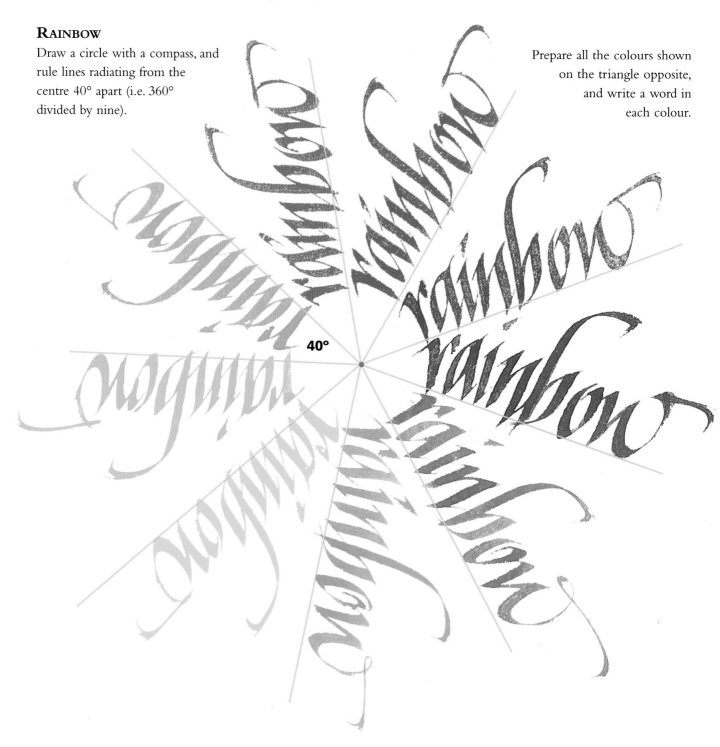

40°

THE COLOUR TRIANGLE

It's easier to understand the relationships and dependencies of colours in the colour wheel if you look at them in a triangle.

You need two reds, two blues and two yellows; a good starting set in gouaches or watercolours might be: scarlet and magenta, ultramarine and cerulean, lemon yellow and cadmium yellow. Trace or photocopy the triangle overleaf and paint it using these primary colours.

On each side of the triangle the primaries with the closest 'bias' can be run into each other to make a bright 'secondary' – try it with ultramarine and magenta first and, as they run together, you should get a bright violet in the middle.

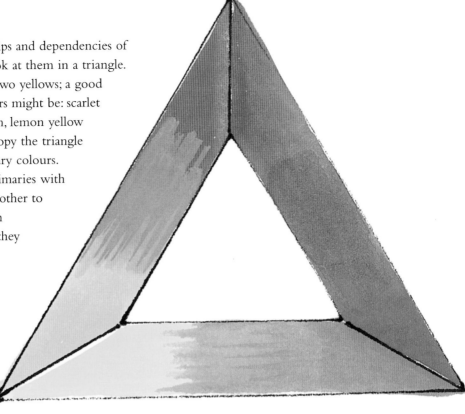

MAKING GREENS

Greens produced from cerulean and lemon, as used in the triangle (i.e. colours which are closest to each other), are bright colours. Duller greens can be made by using the blue and the yellow which are farther away on the triangle – ultramarine and cadmium yellow.

DULLER COLOURS

Mixing secondary colours from primary colours which have their bias away from one another results in less bright, subtler colours. See here how blue and red don't always make violet – particularly when they are made from the blue and red which each have secret yellow in them.

COLOUR THEORY

Colourful calligraphy captivates and excites the eye. Colour
can add mood to your poem, brighten a greetings card, pull
the attention of passers-by to your poster. It can also look
terrible if unhappy combinations are put together, and that's
why beginners often find colour confusing.

The secret is to get to know the three colour families, and why their 'offspring' are the colours they are! At the very least that will help you to decide which colour will look best on your pale blue paper, or why the colours you have mixed have gone unexpectedly brown.

Even if you never want to mix colours (and paint manufacturers provide a bewildering quantity of ready-made hues for our convenience), nevertheless you'll save yourself a lot of trouble if you understand the reasons why some colours work well together and others don't.

All those colours of gouache and watercolour paints are there for your convenience, and if you frequently need to use, say, a deep reddish brown because it's the exact colour you need to match the cover of the memorial book into which you regularly inscribe names, then buy it.

If you need that colour only occasionally, then you can mix it for yourself, along with many others, from a small set of basic colours.

BRIGHT COLOURS

The basic colours are red, yellow and blue, and they are known as the 'primary colours'. You actually need two kinds of each of them. This is

because most colours have a bias towards another colour, and we get the best mixes if we learn to exploit those biases.

So you need to mix together a blue with secret red in it (ultramarine) and a red with secret blue in it (such as rose madder or magenta) to make a bright violet colour. This mixed colour is called a 'secondary' colour, because it is the product of two primaries. Think of it as the offspring of those parents.

USING THE TRIANGLE

Here is a triangle for you to photocopy or trace onto thick paper; if you have the right paints, try mixing them to copy the colour triangle shown on the previous page.

Actually trying it out will help you to understand colour theory. Look how the colours are arranged; parents ultramarine and magenta are mixed together to produce violet. The other two sides of the triangle show the other sets of parents.

The red and yellow with a bias closest to each other result in orange children, and blue and yellow parents with the closest bias produce bright green children. Try mixing some of these

colours for yourself if this is unfamiliar to you.

COLOUR HARMONY

If you are new to colour theory, and want to play safe when choosing colours for your calligraphy, select colours which correspond to one side of the triangle. That way, your design will look colour co-ordinated. If you want duller colours, again play safe and keep all the colours dull as it can be tricky blending bright and dull colours attractively. They can clash. We'll talk about opposites later.

DULLER COLOURS

So, what will happen if you indulge in some cross-breeding? If you want

green, but not the bright spring green that comes from mixing cerulean and lemon, then you should consider a different mix; if you use the other blue, ultramarine, you will introduce some secret red into the mixture, which will effectively dull the colour down to more of a grass green. Dulling down any secondary can be done this way, by using one or both of the 'wrong' parents.

There is another way, too. Mix your bright secondary, then add a touch of its opposite: look at the triangle – green's opposite is red, and by adding a touch of red you'll essentially be doing the same thing as mixing from that other yellow and blue which each had secret red in them.

BROWNS AND GREYS

Brown is not one simple colour. Browns vary from warm rust colours to dark greys; it all depends on the quantities of the original colours used. Of course, there are ready-made browns, made from earth pigments, but here we are concentrating on making our own from primary colours. Mix them from the

primaries, exploring what happens when you have more red in the mix (rust colours), more blue (greyish), or more yellow (greenish).

Keep a note of what you used in your mix, so you can repeat it later. And remember, make sure you mix enough to complete a piece of calligraphy as you'll never be able to match it again exactly.

If you mix all the primaries together in good quantities, you are taking the dulling process to its logical end, which results in a dark grey, nearly black. Try it yourself – you have to keep adding more of one, then another, and it changes from browns to greys to dirty greens as you try to get the darkest result.

This dark-nearly-black is a better colour to use than actual black for writing on top of a colour background; it will be dense but will not kill the colours around it, as black can do.

OPPOSITES

We have already established that if you mix opposites, you will get greys or browns. Put adjacent to each other, still fresh and unmixed, they

have a different effect. Think of red berries on a dark green bush, and you have nature's way of catching your attention. A spot of yellow on an expanse of purple – that's why gold on purple robes looks so effective. Orange sails against a blue sky can be spotted miles away. Using such combinations for an eye-catching effect needs some experimentation – keep the opposite colour as a small amount, as too much will disturb the eye or look crude and jarring. Try a block of text in green, with just one word picked out in red, for example.

For advice on how to use watercolours, turn back to page 118; for gouaches, see page 130. Once you understand the reasons why colours turn out the way they do, you will find it easier to put together colour combinations which look pleasing, and will be able to get the most out of your paints and inks.

This lettering was produced first and then a watery colour was laid across the bottom with a broad brush, allowing the lettering to 'bleed'.

PAINTED BACKGROUNDS

Here are a variety of effects that you create by applying
painted backgrounds in different ways.

The methods by which you achieve
these painted background effects are
explained in detail overleaf.

1 Graduated wash of cerulean blue
on watercolour paper – note the
slight grainy effect.
2 A sponged texture of cerulean
dabbed over yellow while
still wet.

3 Salt – coarse grains – dropped
onto a wash of two colours and
then brushed off.
4 Variegated wash – several colours
dropped in.
5 Clingfilm texture: a two-colour
wash with clingfilm laid over it
and left to dry.
6 Variegated wash – magenta
and scarlet.

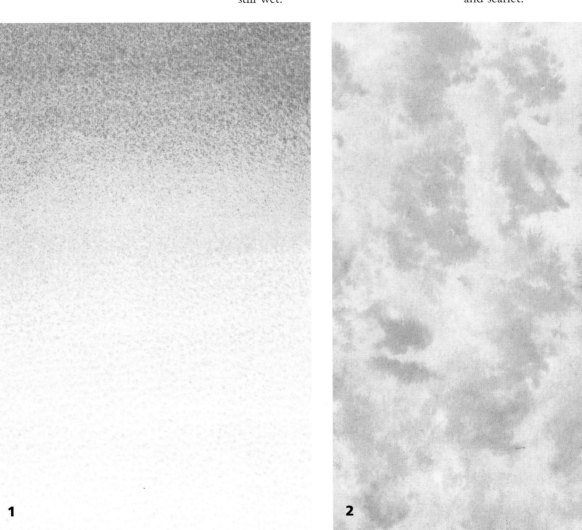

1

2

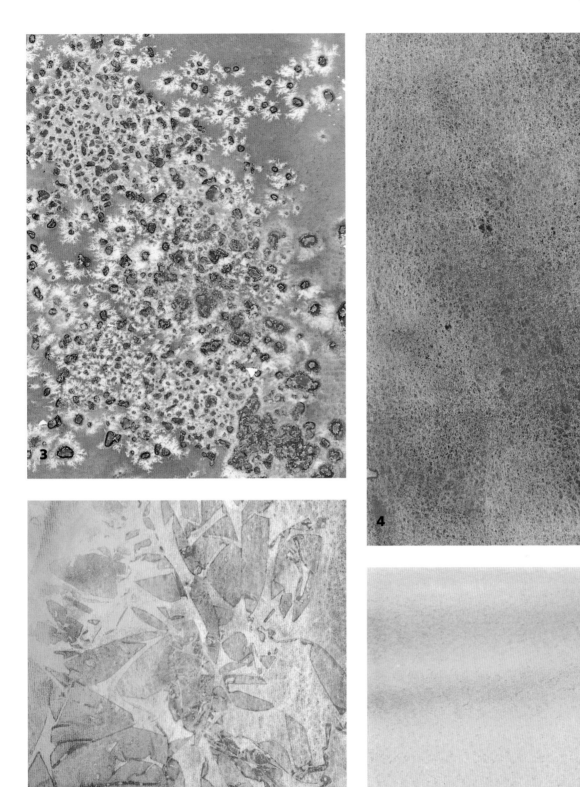

While papers come in all sorts of colours and surfaces, there are occasions when nothing but your own painted background will do. Making your own background can enlarge the range of effects you can create for evocative poetry, for example, or perhaps you simply can't find the right colour 'off the shelf'.

Use either watercolour paints, or inks which will dry waterproof (see pages 114-5), if you are creating backgrounds on which you plan to write. If you use gouache paints, you may have trouble getting crisp writing on top because they deposit a sediment which can make the surface absorbent. Watercolour paints are very thin so they do not have this effect. Best of all, use watered-down acrylic inks because they dry waterproof and thus seal the surface, so it will not be absorbent and it will make a good medium to accept your calligraphy.

EXAMPLES

1 The gouache background has caused the lettering to look crude, with no thin strokes.
2 The watercolour background allows the writing to retain its sharpness.

Try all the examples shown on the previous pages. If you use thin paper it will cockle when it gets wet. This may not matter for trials, but for a piece on which you want to write, you really do need it to be flat, so the paper should be stretched unless it's so thick that it cannot cockle (see page 112 for how to stretch paper).

Once your paper is stretched on a board and dried, prepare your paints. You will need to mix large quantities of colour, and to use a large soft brush to apply the paint. When you

are ready to do this, make sure it is watery and that the brush is well-charged – if it is in danger of dripping, it's well-charged.

If your brush is too small, you will make lots of streaks and the paint will dry out too quickly.

AN EVEN, FLAT WASH

The trick for getting an even colour wash is to slope the board with the paper on slightly, and to apply the paint with a consistently even movement. Start at the top, apply paint right to left, recharge the brush, apply left to right, recharge etc, keeping a bead of wet paint moving down the page. Don't go back over any of it, or you will leave a mark.

GRADUATED WASH

Make this in the same way as the flat wash, except that you should recharge the brush with more water, not more paint, so that it becomes more diluted as you work down the page. Slope the board to encourage the colour to spread downwards. See illustration 1, page 126.

SPONGING FOR TEXTURE

Use a small piece of bath sponge, or, better still, a piece of natural sponge to obtain this textured effect. First spread one colour all over the page – you can use a brush or the sponge for this. Then change the colour, and dab the sponge into the new colour; squeeze it out so that you can

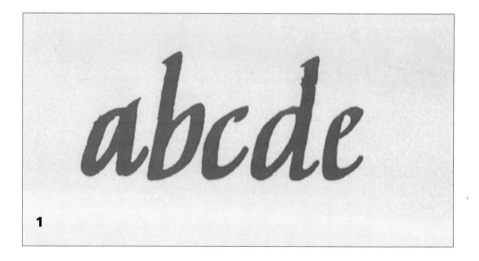

1

2

control the amount of colour you are applying – add more if it's too dry. Dab the sponge all over the paper until you have achieved the effect you want. See illustration 2 on page 126.

SALT TEXTURE

This makes an exciting effect, but the surface is rather difficult to write on as it will be rough, even after the salt has been brushed away. Use coarse grain salt, and sprinkle it onto the wash while it is wet.

You may need to experiment to see just how wet it should be – it's right when you see the salt sucking up the colour straight away! Leave it to dry completely before brushing off the salt. See illustration 3 page 127.

VARIEGATED WASH

This can mean anything – and it's never repeatable! You can achieve some exciting effects by using more than one colour. Of course, a great deal depends on your choice of colours because they will mix on the paper. If you are inexperienced in colour mixing, see pages 122-5.

If you are planning to write on top of the background, it is best to restrict your palette, or it will be too busy to allow any text to show up. Select a main colour and wash that on as you would a flat wash, but without the need to be so careful to get it even. Add other colours while the main colour is still wet. Remember to keep the brush dripping wet. See illustrations 4 and 6, page 127.

CLINGFILM TEXTURE

For a cracked or frosty effect, plastic wrapping film is an ideal tool. First apply your wash, then while it is still wet all over '(wet it again if it has dried), apply the film in an uneven, crinkly layer so that it can be moved about on the paint; twist and drag it about to create the desired pattern.

Leave it to dry – this could take some time as the film inhibits evaporation! When it is dry, remove the clingfilm – the background should look like cracked ice. See illustration 5 on page 127.

GOUACHE PAINTS

Designers' gouaches are the calligrapher's choice for finished
work – they give an even finish on white paper and are
opaque so that you can write on top of other colours. Here is
a project to try on white or on coloured paper.

PROJECT

QUOTATION WITH LEAF PRINTS

You will need

- Selection of leaves with a strong vein structure
- Gouache
- Dip pen
- Good quality paper, white and coloured
- Ruler, pencil, eraser
- Plain white tile
- Ink roller
- Kitchen roll

1 First experiment with the colours you wish to use. For this ginger colour, mix a violet-red with an orangey-yellow; you will get various versions depending on the relative amounts you use. Try it out in the pen to check for consistency and to decide which colour you prefer.

2 Rule up for two lines of text and write it carefully. Make sure you leave plenty of space on the left for the leaf prints.

3 To print the leaves, you need some small leaves that have a pronounced vein structure (not waxy ones), a tile, a small roller and some tissues. Squeeze out onto the tile a little of the gouache (the yellow and the red, plus a touch of ultramarine for darker leaves) and roller it out flat. Then place a leaf on the tile and roll the paint onto it. It will probably stick to the roller! Lift it off gently and place it face down on the paper, then press it down using a tissue or kitchen towel. Prise it off and discard – it will probably not survive another printing. Continue the process, changing the balance of colour mixes on the tile so that each leaf carries a different mixture. If it is a hot day, you will need to work quickly before the paint dries, but don't add water as this will make the leaf print blobby.

3

4

4 When you have succeeded with the process on white paper, try a version on coloured stock. Do some trials first to select colours which will show up on and complement the background. Here the text is written in red, not the mixed ginger as that would be too similar to the paper colour.

GRADUATED COLOURS

Gouache is ideally suited to experiments with colour change. See overleaf for details of how to do this – the same base colours are used as above: violet-blue, orangey yellow, ultramarine.

1

Good quality designers' gouaches are ideal in the pen. They have some of the colour properties of watercolours (bright, lightfast) but are opaque, so that they can be used on top of coloured backgrounds where they stand out well.

They come in tubes, larger than watercolour tubes of similar price because they have more 'filler' which provides the opacity. As with watercolours, they are labelled with their lightfastness – 'Lightfastness 1' or 'Permanence A' signify those which will withstand display in bright light without fading for the longest time. Reds are the most vulnerable to fading, so check the label if this is important.

HOW TO USE GOUACHE PAINTS

Use a mixing palette and squeeze out about 1cm (0.4in) of paint; if it is a new tube, there may be some clear, runny fluid which has to be disposed of first. Add water to the paint drop by drop – you could use an eye-dropper or add water by the (small) brushload. Mix all the paint evenly, then charge your pen with the colour and try writing with it on a scrap of paper.

If the pen feels resistant, the paint is probably too thick; a consistency of thin cream is recommended: add another brushful of water and try again. Keep repeating this method until the paint flows well from the pen. Of course, you may overdo the watering and find you have made the colour too thin – if that occurs, add a little more paint and start again.

1 Several layers of thinly-written gouache, suggesting grasses, has a final top layer of thicker gouache for the readable text.

WRITING IN GRADUATED COLOURS

Some exciting textural effects can be achieved by writing in more than one colour, and by blending them so that they change throughout the block of text. To achieve this successfully, first choose an harmonious set of colours. Mix up enough of each colour for the whole project, and keep separate brushes for each mixture.

The method of feeding the pen with the various colours depends on your preference, and on the type of pen you prefer. If you are using a reservoir, take care that not too much colour fills it, or you will not obtain sufficiently regular changes. As you write, feed the pen with first one colour, then another; do not change colour after each word, rather try to ensure that a gentle colour change occurs within a word.

Obtaining a regular texture of colour changes takes practice and experiment, so don't be disheartened if your first attempt is uneven.

PROBLEM SOLVING

Blobby writing: the paint may be too thick or the pen is overloaded – wipe it on a cloth.

Colours don't change: you may have too much of one colour in the reservoir, or your colour range isn't sufficiently differentiated to show a change.

Pen won't write: check how tight your reservoir is – this may be restricting the flow.

TAKING OUT MISTAKES

Washing out can be tried in the same manner as with watercolour (see pages 120-121). Alternatively, because gouaches have some surface thickness to them, they can often be successfully scraped off. Try this method: when the mistake is completely dry, protect the rest of the artwork with a sheet of paper with a hole cut in it to expose just the area to be corrected. Take a scalpel-type craft knife with a sharp blade and gently scrape the area with the blade held as flat as possible to the paper.

This avoids the blade digging in to the paper or the point catching in it so making a hole. As some paint comes away, lift it off with a putty eraser, and continue until all is removed.

Provided the paper is thick enough, such scraping can be disguised. Now the surface has to be repaired before you can write on top. Burnish the surface with a smooth tool, such as a teaspoon or a polished stone, until there are no lifted fibres and the surface looks slightly shiny.

If you have any, dust the surface with powdered gum sandarac before writing on top, so as to minimize the chance of the paint bleeding. Add some gum Arabic to the paint for the same reason – the paint will be less inclined to spread.

2

2 When using gouache it is often possible to carefully scrape the surface of the paper to remove mistakes.

3 Overlay of repeated letterforms, in pale to deeper colours of gouache, makes decorative patterning.

3

MASKING FLUID

Masking fluid is a rubber solution used by watercolour
painters for blanking out areas of their picture which they
want to keep white while they cover the paper
with a colour wash.

Calligraphers have found that it has many possibilities as a writing medium; write with it on white paper, paint over it, remove the masked area and the effect is of white writing against a colourful background.

Masking fluid is supplied in a bottle, and most versions are creamy coloured, although there is one which looks grey. The fluid evaporates rapidly, so you must keep the top of the bottle closed; it is best

to decant a small quantity into a paint dish and work with that. Don't use your best paintbrush with this substance, as it leaves stringy, rubbery fragments which are difficult to remove. The fluid can be diluted with water, and you may find you need to add a few drops just to bring it to a writing consistency.

Try writing without a reservoir on your pen; dip it or feed it with an old brush, and write only a few words before cleaning the nib; this is

to avoid the fluid evaporating on the nib and so becoming stringy.

If the writing is too blobby, the fluid may need thinning, or the pen has been overloaded. Keep a cloth for wiping away any excess. It is quite difficult to see what you have written, because the fluid dries transparent! The version which is grey is easier to use in this respect. You will be able to see it more clearly if you position a lamp low down to cast an oblique light.

PROJECT

WRITING A SLOGAN

1 Rule your lines lightly, as you will not be able to erase them without affecting the masking fluid. Test your

1

fluid for writing consistency, then write the chosen slogan. The dry masking fluid will be difficult to see!

When the masking fluid is completely dry (its appearance will change from milky to clear), you are ready to apply a colour wash.

Mix ultramarine to a watery consistency (this is important – if it is too thick, it will go streaky and cover the masked area) and make sure you have a sufficient quantity.

You will need

- Masking fluid and water
- Old paintbrush
- Dip pen without reservoir
- Ruler, pencil, eraser
- Watercolour/gouache/inks
- Wash brush or sponge
- Lots of water
- Heavy-duty paper, e.g. watercolour paper

Fill a brush or sponge so that it is dripping, and spread the colour around generously, covering all the masked area and beyond.

2

2 Put a few dots of vermilion and lemon around the 'threat' area. Note how it goes brown (see colour mixing on page 122). It is interesting how the colour collects around the masked letters, and this characteristic is worth exploiting. Leave it to dry. If you used thin paper, it may have cockled by now; continue this as a trial, but next time use thicker paper or stretch the paper first – see page 112. Once completely dry, remove the rubbery solution by rubbing it very gently with your finger, or you can use a soft eraser.

3 (Left) To achieve a 'reversed' effect of dark writing against a light wash, write with the masking fluid on dark paper (caution: it will be difficult to see your ruled lines) and mix a wash of opaque white/yellows from gouache. The result can be very exciting!

WHITE PAINT ON DARK PAPERS

We are often attracted to a coloured paper and want to use it as a base for calligraphy, but find that its colour is rather too dark for black text to show up on it. Why not use white instead? White on a dark background can look very dramatic.

Achieving an even density of paint from the pen takes some practice. Unevenness shows up, particularly if you need to thin the white to a consistency which will run from the pen comfortably. If you try using a thicker mix, you may have trouble getting crisp writing.

There are several techniques which will help here. If you can obtain it, buy a bottle of 'Bleedproof White'; this is very thick and opaque, and will need some diluting – but keep it as thick as you can. Stir the contents well with the handle of a paintbrush, then use that blob stuck to the end – wipe it onto a mixing dish, ensure the rim of the bottle is clean and close the lid tightly (it dries out easily). Never use this white to mix with another colour – interesting chemical reactions occur!

Add a tiny amount of water – one small brush drop perhaps – then feed it onto your nib. Use a flexible nib so that you can use pressure to control the flow. Adjust the slope of your board too – set it flatter if you want more white to flow, or steeper if it has dropped a blot.

Keep the brush in your other hand as you write, ready to wipe across the nib with almost every stroke, thereby keeping the consistency even and preventing clogging. Try it without a reservoir, fed from the top, or by making a masking tape reservoir (see pages 80-81)

If you cannot obtain Bleedproof White, use a good quality white gouache and add a drop or two of gum Arabic which will help to stop it spreading.

Try all the pen techniques as described above.

PROJECT

NOVELTY CARD

You will need

- Coloured paper
- 'Bleedproof White', or gouache with gum Arabic
- Compass
- Protractor
- Ruler, pencil, eraser
- Scissors
- Creasing tool

Select a paper whose colour suits the message – perhaps a warm red or deep purple? If you choose paper which is very dark, however, you will have problems seeing your pencil lines unless you use a lamp set at a low angle. Alternatively, consider using chalk or pastel (but it must rub off afterwards) to mark the lines – you will need to use a sharp edge.

1 Draw a triangle with equal sides (60° corner angles), mark the centre of each side and draw a line to the opposite corner; where they meet is where you will place your compass point. Use a compass to draw the circle round the triangle. Or trace this diagram, or enlarge it on a photocopier to your desired size. Sketch in where the lettering will go.

1

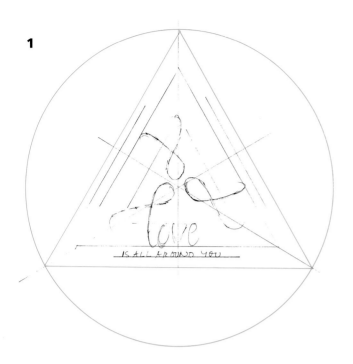

2

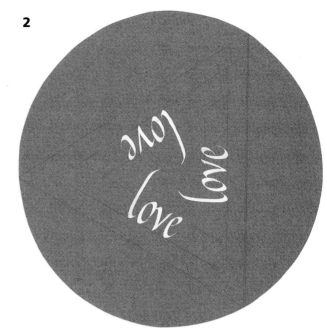

2 Cut out the circle with scissors, and rule lines for the text. Practise writing with the white on an offcut of the paper first, to get used to the surface of the paper and to test the density of your paint.

Write the word 'love' three times, leaving the flourishes until you have established where each word will be positioned.

3 Add the flourishes so that they are all similar and form an even pattern in the middle – they will look best if they don't touch. With a finer pen, write the surrounding text in tiny capitals. This is good practice but it may be tricky to avoid blobbing – the paint may need thinning slightly.

3

4 Make creases using a blunt tool, such as a knitting needle, against a ruler, erase all the pencil lines, and fold the card.

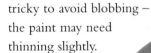

4

IMITATION GOLD AND SILVER

We often want to add the sparkle of gold or silver to our calligraphy and there are many paints and inks which can help us do this. For writing with a pen, you may find that gouaches are best suited as you can vary the consistency to gain optimum flow. Try gold or silver on a small gift container, or perhaps on a label.

PROJECT

A GIFT BOX

You will need

- Gold/silver gouache
- Dip pens, no reservoir
- Stiff coloured paper
- Ruler, pencil, eraser
- Template
- Craft knife and cutting mat
- Blunt tool for creasing

Gold and silver look particularly exciting when used on a coloured paper. Here is an idea for a little gift box on which to try out writing with your metallic paints or inks.

It is very small – if you follow the template shown overleaf – and would hold a tiny gift such as earrings, cuff links or about four expensive chocolates! If you prefer not to measure it out to size, or would like to use different measurements, try enlarging the template on a photocopier.

1 First try out the metallic inks/paints to see which of your pens is the most accommodating; a more flexible pen works best. Try writing some simple text on carefully measured lines.

1

2 Practise writing your text on a curve; you will probably need to make a top line too. With a compass, draw a semicircle of the size you need for the box – this example uses a radius of 75mm (3in).

2

3

3 Select your paper – it needs to be stiff enough to hold a fold well when made up. Draw out the template as shown, following the instructions carefully. Rule the lines for writing. Remember that half of each flap will be obscured when made up, so only write on the portion that will show! Practise writing in the metallic paints/inks on a spare piece of the paper to test for readability.

4 Carefully write your message downwards from the central mark. Leave each section to dry before moving round to avoid smudging.

5 Add some decorative features – design a small pen pattern – and perhaps add a line or two in silver (use a ruler and a fine nib).

6 Make up the box, insert a small gift, and seal it with some gold or silver ribbon (see previous page).

HOW TO MAKE THE BOX

Rule up a square measuring 90mm (3¹/₂in) along each side (to check it *is* square, measure across the diagonals – if both are the same length, it is). Mark on each side where a compass point should sit 25mm (1in) in from each corner. Use a compass to draw the curves – the radius should be such that the curve exactly meets the opposite corner point. These curves should extend 15mm (⁹/₁₆in) beyond each side of the square.

Cut the box out with scissors, or use a craft knife on a cutting mat. Crease the folds using a blunt pointed tool, such as a knitting needle, run against a ruler.

If all this measuring puts you off, just enlarge the template on a photocopier to any size you wish Then you will only need to use the compass to draw the curved line on which you will write.

GOLD AND SILVER INKS AND PAINTS – WHICH IS BEST?

As gold and silver inks and paints are made from finely ground metals, there is a tendency for gravity to take over and for the sediment to settle out of suspension, even separating out in the pen if you are unlucky. If you are using tubes of paint, you only need a small amount squeezed onto a dish.

Then you can stir it rapidly when you see it separating out.

When inks are left standing, they may develop a thick sediment which needs more than shaking to disperse it. If you use the handle of a paintbrush to stir, you will be able to feel just how thick the paint is and break up any lumps. You may well have to keep stirring it while it is being used.

Some inks perform better than others, and manufacturers have used their ingenuity to try to keep the metals in solution, but unless you can follow a recommendation from another calligrapher, you will have to experiment to find one that suits you.

TARNISHING

While genuine silvers will tarnish in time, paints are generally quite reliable; read the label carefully for permanence details if this is important.

TIPS FOR WRITING

A flexible nib is important, to allow enough gold/silver to be deposited on the paper; if your nib has a slip-on reservoir, try using it without the reservoir, feeding the paint frequently onto the top of the nib. If not enough colour is coming from the pen, you may need to thin it with water. If you are sure it is thin enough, try pressing and releasing the nib against the paper before you make the first stroke – this will encourage a deposit of ink to get it going.

Experiment with the slope of your table too, as a flatter angle will encourage more paint to flow onto the paper.

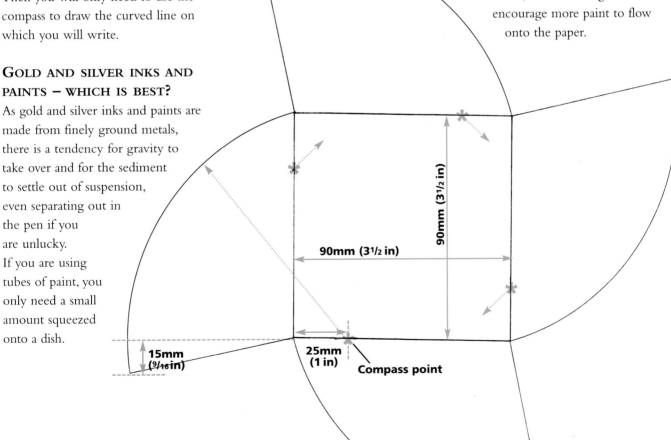

90mm (3¹/₂ in)

90mm (3¹/₂ in)

15mm (⁹/₁₆in)

25mm (1 in)

Compass point

GOLD LEAF

Real gold can be tremendously exciting to use, and is not as
costly as you might suppose.

Those beautiful manuscripts seen in museums, displaying pages of sparkling illuminated letters, are a delight. But that thick layer of gold is a deception. The gold is just molecules thick, stuck onto a raised base. Here are some examples of modern usage of gold on a PVA base.

'ALISON'

Gold diamonds added to a name create sparkle. The PVA was laid on thickly to give a raised effect.

LET THERE BE LIGHT

This uses built-up Versal type capitals in brown ink, with a thin layer of PVA for the gold laid in the spaces between and within the letters. The gold has stuck to the ink in some places, adding to the sparkle.

LOVE

Using thick PVA creates a three dimensional effect for this heart shape within the letter O.

DECORATIVE EFFECTS

Here are some variations showing decorative effects applied to one letter. There is a long and fascinating tradition of decorated initial letters, with many styles employed, such as putting the gold around the letter or making the letter solid gold and creating patterned effects around it. Consider designing a letter for a special gift, and begin by studying the Versals on page 69 to ensure that the letter is perfectly proportioned before you concentrate on the decorative elements.

1 Gold B, painted inside in blue, then with darker blue diamonds painted on top.

2 Gold B, blue rectangle painted around it; freehand decoration painted with bleedproof white and a fine brush – keep the paint very dry.

3 Red B, gold background. Do the gilding first, paint last to prevent gold sticking to the paint. For added decoration, use a blunt point to indent a pattern into the gold.

4 Blue B, gold counter-space. Do the gilding first, then paint the B.

See overleaf for a step-by step method for laying gold.

PROJECT

A DECORATED GOLD LETTER

You will need

- Tracing paper
- Pencil, red pastel, eraser
- White HP watercolour paper
- PVA glue (from a hardware store)
- Paintbrushes, gouaches
- Narrow nib pen
- Transfer gold leaf
- Burnisher or smooth hard object
- Glassine paper or silicone baking parchment

1 First draw your initial letter; design it after studying Versal letters (see page 68), or copy this example.

Trace the outline carefully, turn the paper over and rub pencil across the back. Transfer the design onto good quality smooth watercolour paper by tracing over the design again with a sharp pencil.

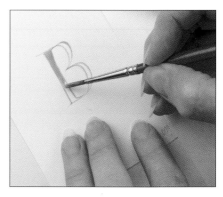

2 Make some watery paint or ink, and work round the outline in thin paint using a narrow pen. When dry, erase the pencil marks. This step ensures that no graphite is present to dirty any delicate painting.

3 Decant some PVA wood glue into a small dish and add a little water – about one third as much in volume. You will need to experiment as not all PVA is the same consistency. Add a little red watercolour to help visibility.

4 With a fine paintbrush, carefully fill in the area outlined. Start with a small amount in the brush to do the edges neatly, then load the brush generously to 'flood in' the central area. Work on a flat table so that it does not puddle at the bottom.

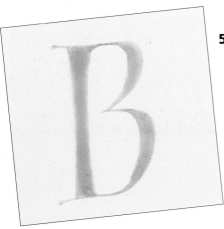

5 Take care not to go over the PVA once it starts to dry or you will make streaks. Leave it to dry.

6 Hold the sheet of gold ready while you breathe heavily on the dry PVA to make the surface damp – five puffs should be enough – and press the gold on firmly using the pad of your thumb. Work small areas at a time, and repeat the process where it has not stuck firmly.

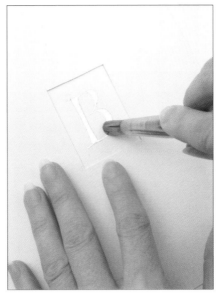

7 When the gold has stuck well to all parts of the letter, polish it to a shine. Use scissor handles, a teaspoon or a smooth stone and burnish it down through a piece of glassine or silicone release paper, which will not scratch the gold.

8 Alternatively, if you have one, burnish directly onto the surface of the gold with a specialist haematite or agate burnisher. Gently brush away any excess gold with a soft brush. Add any decoration (as shown on the previous page).

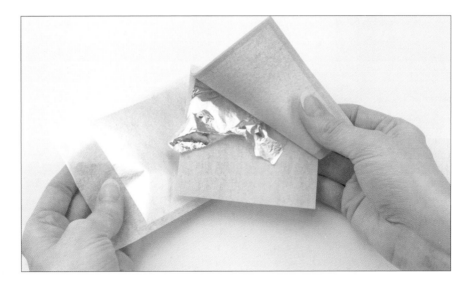

ABOUT THE MATERIALS

GOLD

Real gold leaf comes in books of 25 very thin sheets. It can be 'loose leaf', where it is kept interleaved in the book with pages of tissue paper between, or 'transferred' – attached lightly to a backing paper. This last is ideal for beginners as it is more economical and is not so vulnerable to being blown away.

PVA

This adhesive comes in different strengths – the one for children is too weak for our purposes. Choose your PVA from a hardware store, and select one that is suitable to stick wood. It is a white glue which dries transparent, so it is a good idea to colour it pink (if it shows through the gold it gives extra warmth) to

make it easier to see where we are laying it. It can be laid thickly with a brush, or watered down to write with a pen.

PVA is of course a modern invention, and ideal for beginners as it works in all conditions of humidity, unlike its traditional counterpart, gesso. Gesso is a mix of slaked plaster, white lead, fish glue, sugar and colouring ground together in a thick paste with water and stored in dried cakes. A cold, damp

atmosphere is required for best results in getting the gold to stick to gesso. Modern-day calligraphers have searched for alternatives to suit centrally heated houses and other drier conditions.

While gesso remains superior for a high polish of gold, PVA is an excellent medium with which to learn, and is ideal for urgent jobs which cannot wait for the right humidity to occur!

USING GOLD LEAF AND OIL PASTEL

As you will have seen from the previous pages, gold leaf provides quite a different effect from the gold in gouaches and inks. Gold is generally used in small quantities because of its cost, and as beginners we are often rather afraid of it.

Here is a fun way to use gold leaf which should help to take away the mystery, using the inherent tackiness of oil pastels as the base on which to stick the gold. There is one drawback with this technique – the oil pastel is liable to transfer some of its colour onto anything that it rubs against, so this is not a method to use in a book, for example, where the opposite page will eventually become marked by the offset colour, unless an interleaved sheet is added. See this more as a fun project for ephemeral items.

PROJECT

MAKING A FUN SCROLL

You will need

- Yellow paper, fairly thick – try pastel paper
- 'Transfer' gold, i.e. real gold leaf attached to a backing paper
- Red oil pastel
- Pencil, ruler, eraser
- Red paint/ink
- Dip pens
- Posting tube

MAKING A FUN SCROLL

Yellow paper and red oil pastel are bright, cheerful colours which will enhance the gold, but of course you can select various other colour combinations that please you.

1

*Thank you
for the invitation
to the marriage of*

**ALICE &
ROBERT**

*on 25 June, 2pm
at St Xavier's Church*

1   First of all, practise your writing; imagine you are replying to accept a wedding invitation, and are planning to send a fun scroll reply.

Write all the text, in the sizes you think you will need; the words you will write in the gold should be in a bigger pen. This text will look best if each line is centred, so measure each line and mark the centre.

2   Rule lines on the yellow paper, and also a vertical centre line. Use your trial sheet as a gauge, and mark carefully the widths of each line of text, centring it on the centre line.

Write the red text, leaving a gap for the gold area.

2

3

3 Fill the gap with red oil pastel, making a neat shape and pressing quite hard so that plenty of colour is deposited.

4

4 Place the sheet of transfer gold over the pastel, gold side downwards, and rub with your fingernail on the paper backing until the gold sticks to the pastel. Move the gold sheet and rub some more until enough gold has been deposited.

5 Use a dry pen, and carefully write the names directly into the gold; sorry, but you cannot draw any guide lines! The gold should come off onto your pen, leaving the red underneath showing through.

6 Here is how it should look when completed, ready for rolling and tying up with a red ribbon. Take care to place it in a stout tube if you are sending it in the mail.

5

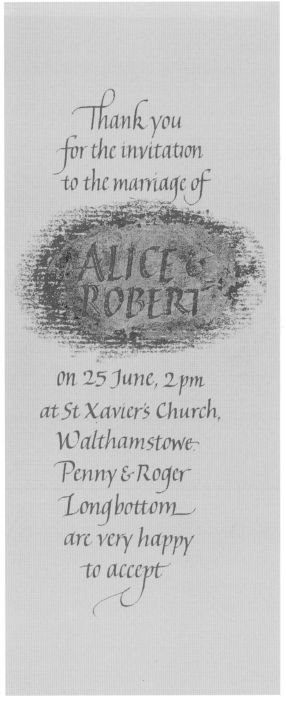

6

DESIGN

Many of us spend a great deal of time in practising writing, and get along well experimenting with a few techniques, but then just do not know how to arrange the calligraphy well on the page. Here are some simple designs to take you through the process of understanding what to look for.

FIND YOUR TEXT

If it is a part of a poem, then the line lengths are decided for you, which can be a problem if they are very uneven; a quotation or piece of prose provides more opportunity for experiment. Here a short quotation has been chosen, and you will see from the next few pages how many variations can be developed from working with just this simple text, each one offering a different emphasis.

When you do select some text, be sure to make note of the author, as you are not trying to pass the words off as your own and the reader may be as interested as you are in the source of the quotation.

The credit can be a valuable element in helping to balance the design, and sometimes it can be the solution to filling a 'hole' in your layout.

Heaven has granted to some
to see on occasion in their mind,
clearly and surely, the whole of
earth and sea and sky. ADAMNAN

1

1 RANGED LEFT

The simplest and most straightforward design is to arrange the text in lines of approximately even lengths, preferably broken at logical points with regard to the sense, and aligned against an invisible left-hand margin. The shorter bottom line has provided us with a convenient spot for the credit.

Heaven has granted to some
to see on occasion in their mind,
clearly and surely, the whole of
EARTH AND SEA AND SKY

2

2 CREATING EMPHASIS

An alternative solution to the problem of the shorter last line is to write it in capitals, which increases the length of the line. This only works if an emphasis naturally falls on these words! Now the line lengths are more even, and we have no space to fit the credit. Where would you put it?

If your instinct is to place it bottom right, think again. That would unbalance the design. Lay some tracing paper over this example and pencil in some ideas. Try tiny capitals along the bottom, aligned left and spread out to the width of the bottom line; see how it would look along the top too.

3 CENTRED, WITH FOCUS

Now we can reassess the text, and think about emphasis again. If we use a larger pen for just one word, this will stand out boldly and give a focus to the design – the eye will be drawn straight to that bigger word. Here, instead of emphasizing the last words, we are focusing on the first. Notice also that this design is centred; so instead of aligning on the left margin, each line has had to be measured carefully in order to start and finish evenly.

The solution for the credit here is to centre it along the top, extending to the same width as the bottom line, so as to enhance the symmetry of the overall outside shape.

A D A M N A N · L I F E   O F   C O L U M B A

Heaven has granted to some
to see on occasion in their mind
clearly and surely, the whole of
earth and sea and sky

3

4 ASYMMETRIC

This takes us back to the four lines as written in example 2, but this time each line is pulled out laterally, making a much wider shape that is in some ways reminiscent of a landscape, which the words suggest.

The placing of the credit has been split, and used to increase the width of the design. Compare this carefully with 2, and notice how the last line achieves more emphasis because it is spread wider across the page. (Did you decide where to put your credit for number 2?).

Heaven has granted to some

ADAMNAN   to see on occasion in their mind

clearly and surely, the whole of   LIFE OF COLUMBA

EARTH AND SEA AND SKY

4

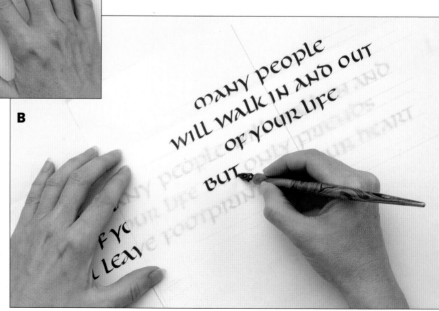

A All the above layouts take time to work out; you can save much of the re-writing if you cut up the lines of text and move them about. Glue them down when you are satisfied with the design. This is called 'paste-up', and a complete project using this method is shown on pages 154–5.

B An alternative method, if you feel you need the practice of re-writing, is to rule your lines on layout paper which is thin enough to see through, and reposition the text as you trace it from the first effort, correcting the spacing and any spelling errors.

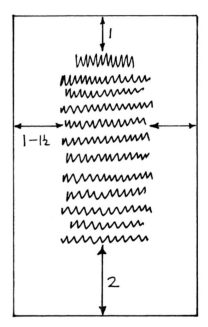

C Once your paste-up or tracing is just how you want it, rule the lines on the 'best' paper, including a vertical centre line if, as here, it is a centred arrangement. Fold the paste-up to show the line you are working on, and fix it above your work while you write. This allows you to check positioning continually as you write.

MARGINS

Margins are not just dead areas – they provide the breathing space for the eye to appreciate the design as a whole. Place strips of dark paper round your design to determine where the margins should be. Start quite close to the writing and slowly pull them away, stopping only when you can see the writing area including the credit, as a distinct shape.

A good 'rule of thumb' is to make your top margin twice the height of the widest interlinear space in your lines of text, then make the side margins up to one and a half times the top margin, and the bottom margin twice the top margin. Play safe and start with generous margins; you can always reduce them later.

DEVELOPING YOUR IDEAS

The designs demonstrated on pages 148–150 illustrate
horizontal or 'landscape' layouts. When you are thinking out
your designs, always consider upright or 'portrait'
versions also.

1 COMMON MISTAKES

This design has several faults. It employs too many changes
from capitals to lower case and back again, making it quite
fussy, but without any one element claiming to be the
main focus. The three blocks compete half-heartedly for
attention. They have all been written with the same size
pen; using a heavier weight or larger pen for one of the
blocks would solve the emphasis dilemma. The overall
shape tapers to a point, a fading out, which is not balanced
by a similar shape at the top.

The credit bears no visual relationship to the main
shape. It would contribute better to the design if it were
centred – or even positioned across the top and written to
the width of the bottom line!

And the margins are demonstrating a sense of paper
economy, rather than good design. Look at the interlinear
space and compare it with the margins (see 'rule of
thumb' explained in Margins on page 151).

2 GOTHIC

This Gothic version is fun. The interline spacing rule has
been broken in order to push the lines closer together so
as to keep an overall density in the text, creating a tall dark
shape. Two contrasting sizes of pen help maintain the focus
on the bottom lines. The credit provides contrast and a
certain light relief at the end. The need for a generous
bottom margin is vital here, to compensate for the
bottom-heavy design.

HEAVEN
has granted
to some to see
on occasion
in their mind,
CLEARLY
& SURELY,
the whole of
EARTH
& SEA &
SKY

xxxxxxxxxxxxx

ADAMNAN

1

2

3 CENTRED ITALIC LAYOUT

The emphasis is near the top, which
is often an advantage in balancing the
design. The actual execution demands
accuracy; because there are so few
words per line, any deviation from
the centre will be noticed. The
interline spaces are less than the
standard to hold the design together.
Note the flourishes on 'to see' – they
are used to widen a narrow line. The
margins may seem generous but tall
designs need plenty of room.

3

4 FREEFORM

When you are entirely confident with your italic, try a freeform version,
written at speed, without many guidelines. This design is only roughly
centred, using more of an asymmetric arrangement which makes the
outside shape more interesting than that of its Formal Italic counterpart.
The contrast is gained with one line written in a much heavier pen
surrounded by lightweight lettering. The flourish at the bottom has
determined the placing of the credit – starting where it finishes, with the
other two lines offset to draw the eye back towards the centre.

4

FROM THUMBNAIL TO FINISHED PIECE

This is how we tackle a project, from start to finish. First select your text. We already have a well-tried text that we will use again, and here we experiment with yet another design, using an asymmetric layout.

PROJECT

A QUOTATION ON A COLOURED BACKGROUND

There are several ways you can plan your designs: a quickly pencilled sketch, a tracing, or a full scale 'paste-up'. Sometimes you may need all three.

1 THUMBNAIL SKETCHES

Thumbnail sketches are useful for first thoughts; remember to include your margins in the drawings, so that you plan with the overall shape in mind. The limitations of such sketches are that we can be over-optimistic when it comes to estimating the lengths of lines in proportion to one another. When this happens, the end product rarely turns out exactly like the sketch. You should try out the most promising ideas with a pen quite quickly, before you get too detailed in your design.

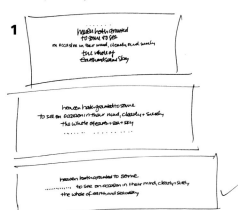

You will need

- Layout paper
- Pencil, ruler, eraser
- Scissors
- Glue stick
- Dip pens
- Good quality paper
- Watercolour or gouache
- Pastels and cotton wool
- Strips of dark paper to check margins
- Fixative spray (optional)

2

ʃ heaven ꞓ aɖamnan ꞓaɖamnan

2 DECIDING ON LETTERFORMS

Having worked out the visual effect you want, next try out a few words using pen and ink. You need to determine what letterform you will use, and how the sizes of main text contrast with the credit, as in this case the credit forms an important part of the overall balance.

Write the whole quotation out once on layout paper, so that you can see how much space it occupies.

3 PASTE-UPS

When you are satisfied with the size and weight of the text, write it all out again and cut the lines out in strips, so that you can lay them on the page and decide exactly how they will be positioned relative to one another.

4 GETTING IT RIGHT

Stick the strips down when you are satisfied with the design, but take care not to be misled by the shadows created by the edges of the paper strips, which may cause you to be too generous with the interline spaces. Take some measurements to check, and also try laying a sheet of layout paper on top to view the whole effect.

The edges can also deceive you when it comes to lining things up vertically; note how the end of the paper with the credit tucks inside the strips above and below it, but the actual text is lined up vertically.

The intention, as you can see from the final design, was to have the text tucked-in, not lined-up. Check for such errors and correct them to avoid disappointment with the final piece. Now do a trial run, a mock finished version,

still on layout paper, so that you can see how your design works. Decide where your margins should be, starting with the 'rule of thumb' (page 151), then check this visually by laying strips of dark paper, or books, rulers etc to indicate the edges. Try pushing them too close, then too far, and you will find that you soon gain an 'eye' for correct margins.

3

4

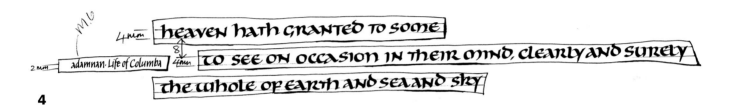

5

5 TRANSFERRING TO 'BEST'

Mix your colour; this is a watercolour mix of scarlet with ultramarine, making a range of rusty browns to purples. When you are ready to write on your chosen piece of paper, rule the lines carefully without pressing too hard – remember you will want to erase them later.

Now take your 'master' sheet containing the paste-up or tracing and fold it so that only the top line of text

shows. Place this above the point where you plan to write. Write the line of text, checking as you go along that you will finish in the right place. Fold the next line over, and continue in the same way. This will help you to check that you are not leaving any words out, and that you are still writing to the same 'tension' (like knitting) as when you wrote the rough.

When the paint is completely dry, gently erase the pencil lines. To make the background, you need blue, pink and grey pastels, and some cotton wool. Apply the colour to the cotton wool, then rub it across the page to deposit the colour. Keep adding more until you are happy with the effect.

Do the same with the other colours. For more texture you might try rubbing the grey directly onto the paper. Trim out the final work leaving generous margins.

SUBJECT FINDER

ALPHABETS

Left/Right Hand

Left-Handers/Right-Handers
18

Materials

Black Inks
116

> PROJECT

A Presentation Bookplate

Coloured Inks
114

See All You Need to Know About Colour 122

> PROJECT

A Fun Bookmark

Gold Leaf
142

> PROJECT

Decorated Gold Letter

Gold Leaf & Oil Pastel
146

> PROJECT

Making a Fun Scroll

Imitation Gold & Silver
138

> PROJECT

A Gift Box

Gouache Paints
130

See Colour Mixing 122, Coloured Papers 100

> PROJECT

Quotation With Leaf Prints

Masking Fluid
134

See Watercolour Paints 118, Gouache Paints 130, Colour Mixing 122

> PROJECT

Writing a Slogan

Tubes or Pans?
120

Watercolour Paints
118

See Colour Mixing 122, Gouache Paints 130, Watercolour Papers 96

> PROJECT

A Decorative Name

White Paint on Dark Papers
136

> PROJECT

Novelty Card

TECHNIQUES

PAINTED BACKGROUNDS
126
See Stretching Paper 112, Watercolour Paints 118,
Gouache Paints 130, Watercolour Papers 96

PEN PATTERNS
22
PROJECT
Red Robin Christmas Card

RULING LINES
20

STRETCHING PAPER
112
See Painted Backgrounds 126
PROJECT
White on Dark Wash

TEARING, FOLDING AND CUTTING
108
PROJECT
Making Greetings Cards

PAPERS

CARTRIDGE
94
PROJECT
A Gift Booklet

COLOURED
100
PROJECT
A Perpetual Calendar

HAND-MADE
104
PROJECT
Making a Collage

PRACTICE OR LAYOUT PAPERS
92
PROJECT
Making a Calligraphy Notebook

WATERCOLOUR PAPERS
96
PROJECT
Making an Alphabet Book